English

D1661943

Exploring the Issues

Berlitz Languages, Inc.
Princeton, NJ
USA

Berlitz Trademark Reg. U.S. Patent Office and other countries
Marca Registrada

ISBN 2–8315–1980–2

Fifth Printing
Printed in Switzerland – June 1998

For use exclusively in connection with Berlitz classroom instruction

Developed by Nick Brieger and Jeremy Comfort of York Associates – 116 Mickelgate, York YO1 1JY in association with John Green TEFL Tapes

Recordings produced and directed by John Green TEFL Tapes 62B Menelik Road, London NW2 3RH

Editing, design and production by Aldridge Press, 24 Thorney Hedge Road, London W4 5SD

Design consultant: Geoffrey Wadsley
Illustrator: Sally Fisher
Picture research: Suzanne Williams

**Berlitz Language, Inc.
400 Alexander Park
Princeton, NJ
USA**

CONTENTS

Dossier 1   Language & Learning   1

1   BREAKING THE ICE
Reading: Fact or fancy? The birth of language   3
Word power: Synonyms and prefixes   4
Word check 1   5

2   YOU, THE LEARNER
Reading: A case for the language doctor?   6
Getting it right: Modal verbs   7
Word power: Word families   7
Word check 2   8

3   WHO'S TALKING?
Listening: Voices and views   9
Sound advice: Accents and origins   9
Word check 3   9

4   HOW TO SAY IT
Interview: Applying the magic   10
Cultural connections: Communication styles   11
Putting it all together: Language teaching survey   11
Word check 4   12

Dossier 2   Food & Drink   13

1   A HEALTHY DIET?
Questionnaire: Are you eating sensibly?   14
Word power: Describing frequency   15
Getting it right: Adjectives with '-ly'   16
Word check 1   16

2   EATING TRENDS
Listening: You are how you eat   17
Getting it right: Language of the senses   18
Word check 2   19

3 EATING CULTURES

Reading: Mind your manners! 20

A question of style: Do and don't – expressing emphasis 22

Word check 3 23

4 DRINKING PATTERNS

Interview: New wines for old? 24

A question of style: Expressing regrets, apologies 25

Putting it all together: Attitudes to food 26

Word check 4 26

Dossier 3 The World of Work 27

1 PROFILES

Reading: Preferred roles at work 28

Word power: Synonyms 30

Word check 1 30

2 TOO MUCH WORK?

Reading: The overworked society 31

Word power: Word building 32

Cultural connections: Attitudes to work and employment 33

Word check 2 33

3 WOMEN'S WORK

Interview: Equal or better? 34

Word check 3 35

4 WHAT'S YOUR LINE

Listening: Jobs and career moves 36

Getting it right: Phrasal verbs 37

Word power: Phrasal verbs 37

Putting it all together: A letter of application 37

Word check 4 38

Dossier 4 Travel 39

1 TAKING CARE

A question of style: Writing styles past and present 40

Reading: Advice for travellers 41

Word power: Classifications 42

Getting it right: Cause and effect 42

Word check 1 43

2 TOURIST TALK

Reading : Signs to remember?   44
Word check 2   45

3 MIXED BLESSINGS

Listening: Tourism – for and against   46
Getting it right: 'Used to'   47
A question of style: Contractions   48
Word check 3   48

4 A BAD IMAGE

Interview: 'If only they'd stay at home'   49
Word power: 'Actually' and 'really'   50
Putting it all together: Holiday preferences   50
Word check 4   50

Dossier 5 · Education

51

1 SCHOOL OF LIFE

Photo feature: The learning experience   52
Getting it right: Using reflexives, reciprocal pronouns 53
Word check 1   53

2 DEAR EDITOR

Reading: Letter from a headmaster   54
Word power: Opposites   55
A question of style: Agreeing and disagreeing   56
Sound advice: Syllable stress   57
Word check 2

3 CAMPUS ORIGINS

Listening: A comparative survey   58
A question of style: Making suggestions   59
Sound advice: Spelling and pronunciation   60
Word check 3   60

4 A NE'ER DO WELL DOES WELL

Interview: Is school worth it?   61
A question of style: Colloquial language   61
Putting it all together: Views on education   62
Word check 4   62

Dossier 6 A Question of Sport

1 SPORTY TYPES

Word power: Personality adjectives   64
Reading: Creating a legend   65
Word check 1   65

2 SPORT FOR ALL?

Listening: Prejudices in sport   66
Word power: Synonyms   66
A question of style: Rhetorical questions   67
Sound advice: Intonation and meaning   68
Word check 2   68

3 PLEASURE AND PAIN

Reading: Fitness - a matter of opinion   69
Getting it right: Using gerunds (verb + '-ing')   70
Word check 3   71

4 GOING FOR GOLD

Interview: For love or money?   72
Sound advice: Regional accents   73
Putting it all together: Your chosen sport   73
Word check 4   74

Dossier 7 International Business   75

1 ROADS TO SUCCESS

Listening: Is it who you know?   76
Getting it right: Using modifying adverbs   76
Cultural connections: Attitudes to appraisal   77
Word check 1   77

2 RULES OF THE GAME

Interview: Dealing internationally   78
Word power: Using 'put' + prepositions   79
Word check 2   79

3 STAR APPROVAL

Reading: Dangerous liaisons   80
Word power: Synonyms   81
Word check 3   81

4 A QUESTION OF HONOUR?

Reading: Big business and the moral maze 82

Word power: Business terminology 83

Getting it right: 'Too' and 'enough' 83

Putting it all together: A business summary 84

Word check 4 84

Dossier 8   Health 85

1 HEALTH VIEWS

Listening: An ideal service? 86

Word power: Talking about problems 86

Word check 1 87

2 ROBODOC?

Reading: Medicine 2010 88

Getting it right: Degrees of probability 89

Cultural connections: Differences in medical practice 90

Word check 2 90

3 HEALTH HAZARDS

Reading: Tobacco – cash crop or killer? 91

Word power: Expressing trends 91

Word check 3 92

4 FRINGE BENEFITS?

Interview: An alternative view 93

Sound advice: Use of idioms 94

Putting it all together: Preparing a topic for discussion 94

Word check 4 94

Dossier 9   The Media 95

1 WHAT SCANDAL?

Listening: Creating a scandal 96

A question of style: Strengths of opinion 97

Word check 1 97

2 LANGUAGE LIMITS

Reading: Expletives deleted 98

Word power: Synonyms 99

Cultural connections: Insults 100

Word check 2 100

3 FORM AND SUBSTANCE

Interview: Image maker   101

Word check 3   102

4 A CHANGED WORLD?

Reading: Communacopia   103

Getting it right: Linking words   104

Putting it all together: A publications review   106

Dossier 10   The Environment   107

1 HERE IS THE NEWS

Listening: Hurricane! A radio report   108

Getting it right: Possible and impossible   109

Word power: Verbs of speaking   110

Word check 1   111

2 BEING AWARE

Questionnaire: How green are you?   112

Word power: Contractions   113

Word check 2   113

3 THE RIGHT OF REPLY

Reading: Sermons or survival?   114

A question of style: Direct and indirect questions   115

Word power: Suffixes '-able' and '-ible'   116

Word check 3   116

4 A HEALTHY BALANCE?

Interview: To add or not to add?   117

Word check 4   118

Dossier 11   The Law   119

1 ORIGINS OF LAW

Reading: Organizing Adamsville   120

Word power: Nouns and adjectives '-ics' and '-ic'   121

Word check 1   122

2 PRACTICES OF LAW

Reading: How fair is the jury system?   123

Getting it right (1): Structuring complex sentences   124

Word power: Legal terminology   125

Getting it right (2): Punctuation   125
Word check 2   126

3   LEGAL SYSTEMS
Listening: Constitutions and procedures   127
A question of style: Expressing emphasis   127
Word check 3   128

4   CRIMINAL MASTERCLASS
Interview: White collar crime   129
Word check 4   130

Dossier 12   Entertainment   131

1   WHAT'S ON TV?
Listening: Pleasing the people?   132
Getting it right: Expressing likes and preferences   132
Word power: Describing programmes   134
Word check 1   134

2   MUSICAL TASTES
Interview: From classics to jazz   135
Sound advice: Silent consonants   136
Word check 2   136

3   FUTURE TRENDS
Reading: The electronic circus   137
Word power: Modifying adverbs   138
A question of style: Formal and informal vocabulary   139
Word check 3

4   A GOOD READ
Questionnaire: Fact or fiction   140
Cultural connections: Favourite writers   140
Word check 4   142

Dossier Key   **143**

Acknowledgements   *241*

PREFACE

Exploring the Issues is designed for the advanced student of English and is to be used in the classroom in connection with live Berlitz instruction.

The program consists of a student book and three audio cassettes. The book is divided into 12 chapters, called "dossiers," covering areas of general interest, such as the environment, education, health, and the media.

At the end of the book there is a key which contains transcriptions of the recordings and answers to the written exercises.

The accompanying cassettes contain a mixture of authentic and scripted material, and are intended to be used both in the classroom and for home review.

We are happy to add *Exploring the Issues* to the body of Berlitz instructional materials and welcome any comments or suggestions for improvement.

1 Language & Learning

Verbal communication distinguishes humans from other animals. But the origins of human language have always puzzled linguists. Did language evolve from animal communication? Or was there a sudden and spontaneous outburst – a linguistic 'big bang'?

Other questions arise: Why are there so many different languages spoken round the world? Do these languages share one common ancestor or are there different roots?

And finally, what about learning a language? Is this based on natural talent or sheer hard work? What are the keys to success?

In this dossier we'll discuss some of these questions and introduce you to the materials that you will be working with in this course.

Features

1. Breaking the ice:
   Fact or fancy? The birth of language

2. You, the learner:
   A case for the language doctor?

3. Who's talking?
   Voices and views

4. How to say it:
   Applying the magic

1

Getting started

This 'ice-breaking' activity is divided into two stages: getting information and reporting information.

- First, ask your partner* questions.
- Make notes on the answers and information given.
- Then report back your findings to the rest of the group.

1. Professional

Find out your partner's
- name
- present job
- present company or institution
- company's activity
- job responsibilities
- previous jobs

2. Personal

Find out about your partner's
- home
- family
- leisure activities
- favourite food and drink

3. Language and learning

Find out the following about your partner
- languages learnt at school
- previous language courses
- reasons for learning English
- results expected from this course

* Throughout the book, the term "partner" refers to another student in group instruction; in private instruction it refers to the teacher.

① Read ⟶
- students report
- corrections.

Fact or fancy? The birth of language

Just as physicists ponder the origins of the universe, so linguists reflect on the origins of language. Here are some popular nineteenth-century theories, which were later given derisive names to suggest their essence as well as the attitudes of their critics.

1. The Bow-Wow Theory
Language grew out of man's attempts to imitate natural sounds. This can be compared with observations of infant behaviour. The infant calls a cow 'moo', copying its sound. The logical development of this theory is that man's first words would have been onomatopoeic or echo words, for example, sneeze, bump, grumble.

2. The Pooh-Pooh Theory
Language originated from the spontaneous human cries: of recognition ('ah'), surprise ('wow'), joy ('ooh' or 'mm') and disgust ('ugh').

3. The Goo-Goo Theory
This theory drew on the others and held that any sound consistently uttered with purpose and meaning will, with the passage of time, come to be consistently understood as having that meaning.

4. The Ding-Dong Theory
Originally proposed by Greek philosophers, this theory suggested that language emerged mystically. As each entity appeared on the face of the earth, it got its own unique name. So, when man first encountered dog, he said 'Dog' and that's how it got its name.

REALLY, IT WAS JUST A LITTLE MISUNDERSTANDING, THAT'S ALL!

5. The Ta-Ta Theory
People's earliest communication was by gesture. At a later developmental stage these gestures were regularly accompanied by movements of the mouth. At the final stage, when it was no longer practical to use the hands for gesture because they were occupied with some other activity, humans learned to modify the air blown through the mouth and nose to make understandable sounds.

6. The Sing-Song Theory
Human speech emerged from the musical expression of emotions. So, the melodious chants used in primitive courtship rituals between men and women were later extended to display other emotions. And from these grew the richness of human speech.

Read through the feature article above and answer the questions which follow:

1. Read Q's —7
2. Read text.
   vocab.

1. Which theories relate the origins of human language to animal sounds?   Theory 1
2. Which theories relate these origins to vocal human behaviour?   Th. 2,3 6
3. Which theories relate these origins to non-vocal human behaviour?   Th. 5
4. Which theories claim human language emerged spontaneously?
   Th 4

3

Discussion

- Which of the theories do you find convincing?
- What are the origins of your language?
- What family of languages do you think it belongs to?
- What are the main differences between your own language and English?

Word power

The words *imitate* and *copy* are **synonyms**; they have the same or similar meanings.

Find synonyms in the reading text for these:

1, Do → Pair work.

2, Practice

one person says statement one uses other word

instantaneous	*spontaneous*	prehistoric	*primitive*
alter	*modifies*	magically	*mysteriously*
distaste	*disgust*	uniformly	*consistently*
derive from	*originate*	movement	*gesture*
delight	*joy*	comprehensible	*understand.*

The **prefixes** *un-, in-, im-, ir-, il-, dis-* and *mis-* are used to make negative forms: *natural – unnatural*.

What prefixes will make the following words from the text into negatives?

1. Do

2. practice

un	popular	*il*	logical
in	human	*ir*	regularly
im	practical	*dis*	appear
non	musical	*in*	consistently
mis	understood	*in*	famous

group question with vocab?

Getting started

1. Read

There is one feature which differentiates human language from the communication systems used by animals: Language has to be learned. If language were innate, then we wouldn't have to learn it, there would only be one language and all of us would speak alike. This is not the case. But how do we learn language?

2. Rod
3. vocab
4. Question

THE AMERICAN PSYCHOLO-GIST **B.F. SKINNER** believed that children repeat the sounds they hear around them and then link them to meaning. This model presupposes that the brain is a passive black box which receives sounds as input and produces similar sounds as output.

THE AMERICAN LINGUIST **NOAM CHOMSKY** disputed this view. He believed that the brain plays a more dynamic role. His model assumed that each of us is pre-programmed to learn language. So, according to the linguistic community, the brain receives sounds, interprets them, deduces the appropriate language rules and then applies these rules to produce speech.

⑤ →) • How do you think you learned your first language? Was it by repetition? Or was it by subconsciously applying the rules?

A case for the language doctor?

LANGUAGE PLATEAU

I seem to have reached a plateau with my language – especially vocabulary. On the one hand I recognize and understand quite a wide range of words and expressions; but, on the other, I find it difficult to use these words. I am quite comfortable with the words I know, but I feel that I can't explain my ideas as I'd like. Often I have to go round in circles to say what I mean.

Anders from Sweden

WEAK LISTENING

I can read quite well in English – even authentic texts. But my listening is much weaker…

Mariluz from Argentina

JEALOUSY!

I have to attend a lot of business meetings with participants from different countries. It's very strange how some nationalities manage to express their ideas even though their English is not very fluent. I am quite jealous.

Anna from Germany

NOBODY UNDERSTANDS ME …

I'm really embarrassed about my accent in English. When I speak, nobody understands me the first time. And then I can see that they have to concentrate very hard to follow what I'm saying.

Yuki

MISUNDERSTOOD

The grammar of English was really difficult for me to learn. I still can't use it correctly all the time, but people say they can understand me.

Fa'ad from Oman

Learning a second or foreign language is certainly different from learning a first language. Look at the above comments from advanced learners with different language backgrounds.

If these comments were addressed to a language doctor, these are the sorts of replies they might get.

But which reply goes with which comment?

1. Dear ...Fa'ad...
Remember that words, not rules are the primary carriers of meaning. So don't worry too much if you can't manage to use all the rules correctly all the time.

2. Dear ...Anna...
Your interesting cross-cultural observation illustrates the nature of effective communication. It isn't necessarily the words that convey your message, but the *way* you convey them.

3. Dear ...Yuki...
Pronunciation habits are very difficult to change, but, of course, you should aim for comprehensibility. My view is that your accent is a part of your cultural identity. So be proud of it.

4. Dear ...Anders...
This is a typical problem for advanced learners. My advice is to set yourself a target – a realistic one – for the number of new items you want to learn each week. Build up your own personal list by writing the new words in it. And then make sure that you use them.

5. Dear ...Mariluz...
All skills need practice – the more you practise, the better you'll become. Don't expect to be able to follow every conversation. Start by listening to educated native speakers, for example, news presenters. They are usually good models.

[handwritten margin notes: 2. Read answers 3. Read aloud gr, decided and why?]

Discussion

Discuss the main difficulties you face with the English language.

- Which of the four skills (listening, speaking, reading, writing) present you with the greatest problems?
- Discuss an action plan to improve your knowledge/performance in each of these areas.

Getting it right

Look at the verb phrase in the following sentences:
*I always think I **should have understood** them.*
*I feel it **must have been** an effort.*

In each sentence there is a modal verb *(must, could, should,* etc.) and a past infinitive *(have* + past participle).

Rewrite the following sentences, using the modal verb given in brackets, and a past infinitive.

1. It is possible I studied last year. *(might)*
2. It is possible that language grew out of people's attempts to imitate natural sounds. *(could)*
3. It is obvious that people's earliest communication was through gesture. *(must)*
4. It is impossible that you learnt English as a foreign language. *(couldn't)*
5. My advice would have been to practise more and study less. *(should)*

Now write three things that you *could have done* or *should have done* to improve your language.

Word power

One way of increasing your word power is by building 'word families'. Complete the following table.

Noun	Adjective	Verb
....	....	believe
....	weak	....
expression	....	....
....	....	produce
advice	....	....
....	....	repeat
....	basic	....
....	....	apply
practice	....	....
....	....	recognize
observation	....	....

7

Now complete the following sentences using the words from your word table.

1. According to the Skinner model, language is learnt by
    ....

2. The Skinner model cannot explain how children are able to
    combine words to make .... they have never heard
    before.

3. One rule in language learning is: The more you .... the
    more fluent you'll become.

4. At an advanced level it is .... to try to extend your
    vocabulary, since words are the main carriers of meaning.

5. Learners often regard their foreign accent as a ...., but it
    is rather a sign of their language origin.

Learning long lists of unrelated words is difficult for many learners.
Try to be realistic and systematic about your vocabulary learning.

*   First, set a realistic target, say, ten new words a week.

*   Second, organize your vocabulary learning around themes so
    that you focus on related words. For example, take a piece of
    paper and write a topic in the middle, say, 'language'. Now
    circle it. Then write around it the key words that you already
    know. Then add ten new words from this dossier that you want
    to remember.

You can use the same approach for vocabulary learning for each
dossier in this book, as well as other themes. You could even build
up your own dossier of themes in a folder for later reference.

WORD CHECK 2

to differentiate show the difference
innate inborn
to dispute argue against
to deduce draw a conclusion from the
    information given
to reach a plateau arrive at a level from
    which it is difficult to progress further

spy person who keeps secret watch in
    order to get information
target objective, aim
to transmit communicate to others

Getting started

I'm studying English to improve my understanding of the Anglo-American culture.

I'd like to be able to talk about the same topics in English as I do in French.

1. Read

2. ask?

These two people have different reasons for learning English. What are your reasons?

Voices and views

— Students should take general Notes

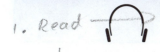

1. Read

Listen to the five extracts from the dossiers and link each extract to one dossier.

*① *

② . General Q's

— some vocab

Extract	Dossier
1.	A Question of Sport
2.	Travel
3.	The World of Work
4.	The Law
5.	The Media

Sound advice

The speakers in the extracts came from a range of geographical backgrounds. Listen again and try to identify their origins. Which are easier to understand; which more difficult?

1. Q's
2. Group questions.

WORD CHECK   3

backwater out of the way place
substance here, importance
to elevate raise above
apartheid political system which
  segregated the races in South Africa

shanty house or dwelling made with only
  basic materials
to hound hunt or pursue
tabloid popular newspaper
splashed all over (the paper) here, given
  great prominence

trains
- education
- fools

press
- politicians
- starts

Getting started

2, Brainstorm

What are the characteristics of a good communicator?

Applying the magic

1, Read

Nigel Lambert is a well-known British actor and performer, who also trains business people for conferences and presentations. He talks about the techniques of language presentation on stage, in formal situations, and in a foreign language.

Listen to the interview and answer the following questions.

Part 1

ask

stop

1. Why do actors need vocal training and technique?
2. What is the particular point of breathing techniques?
3. What helps an actor's body language to come naturally?

Part 2

ask

stop

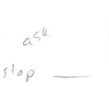

4. What is the main fault Nigel describes in his business clients?
5. What is the key element he points to in effective communication?
6. What key tips does he give for the individual?

Part 3

7. What tips does Nigel give to anyone learning a language?

Discussion

Nigel Lambert described some of the elements needed for effective communication and some ways to develop these skills.

ask

- What skills do you think you need to develop in your own communication?
- How could the approach Nigel described help you in achieving this?

Cultural connections

1. Read ──────➔

The main purpose of communication is to transmit a message. But different cultures place different values on communication. One method for distinguishing between cultures is to divide them into low-context cultures and high-context cultures.

People from low-context cultures:
- are very direct in their communication
- like verbal communication
- place great emphasis on the accuracy of the message
- need all the information in order to make a decision

People from high-context cultures:
- prefer indirectness in communication
- are less dependent on the spoken word and rely more on what is unsaid
- provide information which often lacks essential detail
- use body language and physical proximity to establish relationships

2. Discuss .

Which of the above features describes your culture?

Putting it all together

no

Developing competence in a foreign language is a long-term process involving both study and practice: study to learn the grammar and vocabulary; practice to develop communication skills. Given these factors, how effective is foreign language teaching in your country?

You can answer this question by working on a project to collect information from learners and teachers. On the next page you'll find instructions on how to proceed.

1. Prepare a questionnaire to identify the objectives of teachers and learners of a foreign language. To prepare the questionnaire, write down six possible objectives of learning a language, for example:
   - to learn the grammar
   - to understand the culture
   - to communicate more effectively
   - to travel to the foreign country

2. Carry out your survey by interviewing four people: two language teachers and two adult students. Ask each person to rank in order of priority their objectives of language teaching/learning.

3. Write up your results in a report.

4. Present and discuss the results of your survey.

teenagers

vocab.

teacher

WORD CHECK 4

to harness control
diaphragm muscle which separates the chest and lungs from the lower part of the body
phoney false, unconvincing
paramount importance more important than anything else

to drone on speak monotonously, at length
stilted unnatural
projection actor's method of throwing the voice
fired up enthusiastic
a line here, a phrase, or sentence

1. Read.

Postscript

Misuse of a word or phrase can convey the wrong message!

'If this is your first visit to our country, you are welcome to it.' *Airport sign*

'The lift is being fixed for the next day. During that time we regret that you will be unbearable.' *Hotel notice*

2 Food & Drink

Food and drink are among life's necessities, but their significance goes far beyond mere survival. In religious terms, the Last Supper is central to Christian beliefs; and in order to fulfil the requirements of Islamic and Jewish law, the choice and preparation of particular foods is carried out according to halal and kosher methods respectively.

Food is also linked to social trends. Today's pressurized patterns of work mean that, in many countries, less time is available for a sit-down meal, especially in the middle of the day. So, many people 'graze' or 'snack' – they eat small quantities at frequent intervals, rather than taking an hour or more off work for a substantial meal.

In this dossier, we'll look at some traditional and some modern aspects of eating and drinking.

Features

1 A healthy diet?
You are eating and drinking sensibly?

2 Eating trends:
You are how you eat

3 Eating cultures:
Mind your manners!

4 Drinking patterns
New wines for old?

① Read
② Question
③ Vocab.

13

Getting started

Which of the following sayings reflect your attitudes to food and drink? Do any of them surprise you?

agree?

One should eat to live, not live to eat.
Cicero, Roman orator and statesman (106 - 43BC)

Food is an important part of a balanced diet.
Fran Lebowitz, US writer and columnist

Alcohol wrecks more marriages than sex.
Art Bertoni, US sociologist

Gluttony is an emotional escape, a sign that something is eating us.
Peter de Vries, US novelist

A day without wine is a day without sunshine.
French saying

Everything you see,
I owe to spaghetti.
*Sophia Loren,
Italian-born actress*

Are you eating and drinking sensibly?

This questionnaire tells you about your eating and drinking habits.
Answer YES or NO to the following questions.

	YES	NO
1. Do you generally have your meals at regular times with your family rather than snacking or grazing throughout the day?	☑	☐
2. Do you use polyunsaturated cooking oil and low-fat margarine rather than butter or lard for cooking?	☐	☐
3. Do you drink, on average, less than 2 litres of wine or spirits every week?	☐	☐
4. Does your usual diet include some cereal, fresh fruit and green vegetables on most days?	☐	☐
5. Do you often choose to eat fish rather than red or fatty meats such as beef or pork?	☐	☐
6. For occasional between-meal snacks do you eat fresh or dried fruit or raw vegetables rather than cakes and pies?	☐	☐
7. Do you avoid salted, smoked and pickled foods?	☐	☐
8. Do you take tea or coffee without sugar, and do you rarely take sweet soft drinks in general?	☐	☐
9. Do you limit your intake of coffee to 5 cups a day?	☐	☐
10. Do you drink, on average, less than 4 litres of beer every week?	☐	☐

Evaluation
The more YES answers, the healthier your diet and the more sensible your eating habits.
If you have more than 3 NO answers, you should examine and alter your eating habits.

Discussion

group

1. Compare your answers to the questionnaire and discuss in what ways you think you need to improve your diet.

2. The diagram below shows the results of a World Health Organization survey indicating the percentages of obese middle-aged men and women in various countries.

| 4% | 5% | 3% | 6% | 8% | 9% |
| *Netherlands* | | *Honduras* | | *UK* | |

| 9% | 9% | 6% | 14% | 12% | 15% |
| *Canada* | | *Costa Rica* | | *USA* | |

"Super size me"

- Do you see any particular pattern in these percentages?
- How seriously do you think such surveys should be treated?

Word power

Read — in pairs. — then questions.

Frequency words or phrases tell us how often something happens.

The questionnaire includes a number of words of **indefinite frequency**. They have been placed here in position on a scale which indicates their meanings:

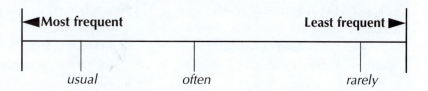

◄ **Most frequent**   **Least frequent** ►

usual   often   rarely

On the next page you'll find a list of words and phrases. Place them in appropriate positions on the scale, as illustrated by the three examples above. You may want to group some words together in the same position.

generally	occasionally	once in a while
rarely	always	never
constantly	seldom	usually
periodically	frequently	often
now and then	normally	scarcely ever
nearly always	infrequently	regularly
hardly ever	almost always	sometimes

whats the question!
How often?

Now write six sentences about your own eating habits, using words or phrases from the above list.

Getting it right

Practice adverbs + Adjectives

Adjectives and adverbs can usually be distinguished from one another by their form, but there are some exceptions. Words like *early*, *fast*, and *yearly* are used as both adjectives and adverbs. Which of the following sentences are grammatically correct?

1. My weekly diet includes fish at least once.
2. As usually, we had chicken yesterday.
3. At present I am following a monthly diet plan to try to lose weight.
4. We have noted a constant increasing demand for more health foods.

WORD CHECK   1

sit-down meal   a meal for which the participants sit down

to graze   feed while moving about (usually applied to cattle); see *to snack*

to snack   eat small quantities of food between or instead of regular meals

gluttony   habitual excess in eating or drinking

polyunsaturated   describing oils and fats in food which are necessary in small quantities for a healthy diet; good sources are vegetable oils, olive oils, soft margarines, nuts, and oily fish

lard   animal fat used in cooking which is high in saturated fats and therefore considered unhealthy

pie   a food consisting of meat or fruit topped with pastry

to pickle   soak in a solution of salt or vinegar for preservation

intake   consumption

ample   more than adequate   *amount*

obese   grossly overweight

Getting started

- What factors have contributed to the increase in snacking?
- Is snacking common in your country? What snack foods are sold?

You are how you eat

 Listen to the extract taken from a radio discussion about food. As you listen, complete the programme notes below.

1 Twenty years ago the modern eating era began.
   Ten years later   out went ___saturated fats___ , ___salt___ and ___sugar___ : in came ___fibre/fibrous food___ , ___fresh food___ and ___vegetables___
   Junk foods   contain ___few___ or ___no nutrients___ apart from ___energy___ .
   Sweets   contain no ___vitamins___ , no ___minerals___ and no ___protein___ .

2 Fast food   describes snacks which are ___already prepared___ or ___cooked___ to order within minutes so that they can be consumed ___on the premises___ or ___taken away___
   3 examples: ___burger bar___ , ___baked potato outlet___ and ___sandwich shop___ .
   But fast food   may result in a high intake of ___salt___ , ___energy___ and ___fat___ .

3 First, Helen   doubts that any snack food outlet provides a ___truely balanced diet___
   Second, Helen   is concerned about the way that snacking is changing ___social aspects of eating___
   Helen   believes eating should be more than ___just a functional activity___

Discussion

Do you agree with Helen that eating is more than just a functional activity and that snacking is bad for your health?

Consider the following sentences taken from the listening passage:

> *But to many listeners energy sounds positive.*
> *Of course, they taste delicious and are hard to resist.*
> *Our food looks good.*

Getting it right

There are five senses: sight, hearing, smell, taste and touch. Each sense has three activities associated with it.

Intentional activity: *We looked at the menu.*
Unintentional activity: *I've just seen a fly in my soup.*
Describing the current sensation: *The main course looks good.*

Sense	Intentional activity	Unintentional activity	Current sensation
sight	look at (a static object)	see	look
	watch (a moving or changing object/activity)		
hearing	listen to	hear	sound
smell	smell	smell	smell
taste	taste	taste	taste
feel	touch/feel	touch/feel	feel

Notes:

1. We use **well** to describe health and **good** to describe positive attributes:

    He looks/feels very well. (healthy, not ill)
    The future looks very good. (positive, not bad)
    The material feels very good. (high quality, well-made)

2. We use the simple present, not the present continuous for unintentional activity and current sensation verbs:

    Do/Can you see that fly in your soup? (Not: Are you seeing …)
    The salads look very appetising. (Not: are looking …)

Each of the sentences below contains a mistake. Underline the mistake and then write the correct form.

1. After work I like looking at television.
2. I am smelling something strange. Is it coming from the kitchen?
3. I can recommend the restaurant. All our meals tasted well.
4. If you watch over here, I'll show you something interesting.

Now complete the following sentences by putting an appropriate verb in the correct tense.

1. I can .... footsteps. They .... like Pete's.
2. Did you get a chance to .... this report on eating habits?
3. On my way through the kitchen, by chance I .... some of their ingredients.
4. From what I saw, most of their cooking equipment .... very old-fashioned.
5. There's a gas leak; you can .... it everywhere.
6. Just .... that noise; that food-processor needs repairing.

Role Play

Imagine you are presenting a radio programme. Discuss two or more of the following propositions in an appropriate style:

1. We pay far too much attention to food and diet.
2. We spend too much money on food.
3. We should all grow fat and be happy.
4. Food and drink are responsible for many social problems.

WORD CHECK 2

era period

inextricably so closely bound that it cannot be separated

pundit learned expert or teacher

to have a go at *(BrE colloquial)* criticize

nutrient something which provides nourishment

to imply suggest

excess more than is required

confectionery sweets

to advocate recommend

to put in a word for support

derogatory negative, insulting

ubiquitous widespread, found everywhere

outlet place or shop where something can be bought

constituent part or element

inherent characteristic

wholesome healthy

ambience surroundings

entrenched fixed

core centre, heart

wellbeing state of being well in terms of health, happiness and prosperity

Handwritten annotations:
identity + language
culture + identities.
culture + language
visual arts + aesthetics.

1920's era
Post-War era.

Corrections

parts of English class - Speakers   Media
good health
Prince Charles
Camillia   Public
exercise

English
Internet

HM?
Saturn?
- Health Diet?
- Good English Class?
linked.
social rules.
respect
idea are entrenched.
Milk.
"legal"
college
show
eat/drink in
what kind of food provide nutrients
Camilla.
why? what imply?
healthly life style?

19

Getting started

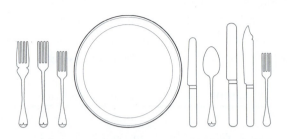

Manners maketh man.

Motto of Winchester College and New College, Oxford

On the Continent people have good food;
in England people have good table manners.

George Mikes, Hungarian-born writer and humorist

1. Read
2. Discuss Breifly

Mind your manners!

Read the extracts and answer the questions.

1

Table Manners and Social Class

The food you eat often indicates what class you are, the way you eat it, namely your table manners, does so almost as much.

The upper classes, for example, don't have any middle class inhibitions about waiting until everyone else is served, they start eating the moment food is put in front of them. This stems from the days when they all dined at long baronial tables, and if you waited for fifty other people to be served, your wild boar would be stone cold. Nor would Harry Stow-Crat* comment on the food at a dinner party, because there's no point in congratulating your hostess on something that's been cooked by someone else. Equally, if he knocked his wine over, he wouldn't apologize because, traditionally, there would be a fleet of servants to clean it up.

(From *Class* by Jilly Cooper)

* Read this name out loud to appreciate its meaning!

2 Manners and the International Manager

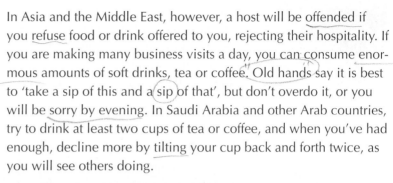

In the United States, you may or may not be offered a cup of coffee at the beginning of a business meeting, and chances are that it will come in a Styrofoam cup or odd mug. Furthermore, nobody cares whether you drink coffee or not.

In Asia and the Middle East, however, a host will be offended if you refuse food or drink offered to you, rejecting their hospitality. If you are making many business visits a day, you can consume enormous amounts of soft drinks, tea or coffee. Old hands say it is best to 'take a sip of this and a sip of that', but don't overdo it, or you will be sorry by evening. In Saudi Arabia and other Arab countries, try to drink at least two cups of tea or coffee, and when you've had enough, decline more by tilting your cup back and forth twice, as you will see others doing.

Generally, do not take food or drink until specifically invited to do so. The fact that it is set before you on a table is not necessarily an indication that it is polite to help yourself. In Indonesia, for example, you must be invited to taste the food that has been sitting in front of you during the conversation, and then you should, without haste, savor the food and prepare to leave. The invitation to eat is a sign that the meeting or visit is drawing to a close.

(From *Going International* by Lennie Copeland and Lewis Griggs)

3 Some Dos and Don'ts around the World

Australia
Dinner is usually about six o'clock. Come a half-hour early or be on time, but never late. Guests sometimes bring flowers, wine or beer, not usually gifts.

Brazil
Some invitations will tell you to come 'American' or 'airport' time, which means on time; otherwise try to be a bit late so as not to embarrass your hosts by arriving before they are ready.

People's Republic of China
Most entertaining will be at restaurants or banquets. Each guest may be seated and served by the host; do not serve yourself. Eat sparingly, as there are many courses. The host will signal the end of the meal, and you should depart promptly.

Egypt

Lunch is the main meal rather than dinner, usually from two to four o'clock, and you may be invited for the day. You should arrive around eleven or twelve. Wash your hands before the meal and after.

Italy

Dinner may be from eight to ten, sometimes earlier in small towns. You may bring a gift or send flowers afterward, but not chrysanthemums which are used for funerals and grave sites. Hands are kept above table. Compliments on the meal and home are appreciated.

(From *Going International* by Lennie Copeland and Lewis Griggs)

1. In extract 1, what three aspects of table manners does the author point out?
2. In extract 2, what are the author's two recommendations about taking food and drink?
3. From the information given in extract 3, which of the countries pay strict attention to time-keeping in relation to meal times?

Discussion

Every culture has its dos and don'ts for different types of situations.

- Discuss the dos and don'ts of table manners in your country.
- Then draft a set of recommendations for visiting foreigners.

A question of style

Dos and don'ts can be expressed in a range of strengths, from absolute necessities or prohibitions to tentative suggestions. Using the right amount of emphasis is important in conveying the right strength of meaning.

Listen to the three short extracts about eating habits and customs on the recording. Indicate in the box opposite whether the speaker expresses the dos and don'ts forcefully (+), moderately (/) or tentatively (–).

1.
2.
3.

These phrases indicate the following range of strengths:

Forceful   You definitely must/have to/need to …
                      You absolutely mustn't …
                      You are not allowed to/permitted to …
                      under any circumstances/conditions
                      It's completely/totally prohibited/forbidden …

Moderate	(I think) you should/ought to/'d better …
	(I think) you shouldn't/oughtn't to/'d better not …
Tentative	It would be/might be is a good idea to ….
	If I were you, I'd …

On the recording you will hear eight comments about manners in different countries. Write the name of the country and the degree of strength used by the speaker to express the 'do' or 'don't'. The first one has been done for you.

Country	Do/Don't	Strength (+, / or –)
Japan	*Try to use chopsticks*	/
	Say thank you as you leave	
	Talk business over lunch	
	Assume Hindus eat beef	
	Send a thank you card	
	Bring alcoholic drinks	
	Leave soon after eating	
	Eat everything on your plate	

WORD CHECK   3

inhibition   reluctance to do something for social or cultural reasons

to stem from   arise from

baronial   describing a baron, a member of the British nobility

stone cold   absolutely cold

a fleet of   a large number of

Styrofoam   a form of plastic

odd   not belonging to a set

old hands   people with a lot of experience (of) doing something

sip   small quantity of drink

to tilt   move to a sloping position

to savor   taste

Note: A systematic difference in spelling can be seen in words ending in 'our' (BrE) and 'or' (AmE). For example:

BrE: savour, colour, neighbour, favour, labour, humour, harbour

AmE: savor, color, neighbor, favor, labor, humor, harbor

to draw to a close   come towards the end

promptly   right away

sparingly   in small quantities

23

Getting started

diseuss

- How important is food and drink as part of your national culture?
- What drinks are typical of your region or country?
- Are the drinking habits of your region or country changing?

New wines for old?

Steven Burns works for the Wine Institute of California. In this interview he talks about the production of wine in his home state, as well as international drinking patterns and trends for the future.

Listen to the interview and complete the following notes.

Part 1
1. Area of wine production   *One end of California to the other...*
2. Features of the wines
3. Slogan for Zinfandel   *"Life is hell..."*

Part 2
4. Main export markets for the wines
5. Recent changes in drinking habits and attitudes
6. Slogan for red wine

Part 3
7. World-wide trends in drinking habits
8. Slogan for wine 'as a beverage'

A question of style

1) Read.

2) Do →

situations from MAE role plays

Near the start of his interview, Steven said, 'Well, unfortunately, there are fifty-two designated, approved viticultural areas…' Expressing regret or apologizing for something requires great care in choosing the appropriate phrase and intonation.

Link the situations (1-6) in the list below with an appropriate apology (a-f), and then practise saying each apology out loud.

Situation

1. Tell your partner that dinner will be late.
2. Explain to your boss why you missed an important meeting.
3. Tell your neighbour her cat has been run over.
4. Your partner wants to know why you forgot the shopping.
5. You have to postpone an important meeting.
6. You are writing to someone rejecting their job application.

Apology

(a) I'm afraid I've got some really bad news for you …
(b) Well, unfortunately, I …
(c) I'm sorry, but …
(d) I'm sorry to have to tell you that …
(e) I regret to inform you that …
(f) I really must apologize for …

Which of the above phrases are neutral, which formal, and which casual? What other phrases of apology can you think of in each of these three categories? In what situations would you use them?

Discussion

Disc

Steven Burns explained how wine consumption is growing despite a worldwide fall in alcohol consumption. He also stated that wine was now perceived as a healthy beverage.

Are the drinking habits of your region changing? If so, are they changing in the way Steven describes, or in other ways?

Putting it all together

In this dossier we've seen how food and drink are both universal for life, yet highly individual for lifestyle. However, food and drink also make up a multi-billion dollar industry, dedicated as much to providing pleasure as to satisfying basic needs. It was Oliver Twist in Charles Dickens' novel of the same name who astounded the workhouse by daring to ask for more. But what could be more natural? Food, glorious food!

Now it's your turn to collect some information about people's attitudes to food. You should try to get as wide a range of opinions as possible for your project. Here's how you should proceed.

1. Design a questionnaire to collect attitudes to food and eating.
2. Collect the data from about ten people of various ages and from different social backgrounds.
3. Prepare a written report collating the results of your survey.
4. Present and discuss the results of your survey in class.

WORD CHECK 4

viticultural   concerning the growing of grapes, especially for wine

microclimates   regional weather variations

to lay down   here, store wines over a period

varietal concept   method of naming wines after their grape variety rather than the area they come from

bumper stickers   labels with slogans that can be stuck on cars

vintage dated   showing year of bottling

foils   covering for wine bottle tops

organic wines   wines grown with minimal use of chemicals etc.

Postscript

If you have formed the habit of checking every new diet that comes along, you will find that, mercifully, they all blur together, leaving you with only one definite piece of information: French-fried potatoes are out.

From *Please Don't Eat the Daisies*
by Jean Kerr

3 The World of Work

As it has done for the last two centuries, the world of work continues to undergo enormous change, socially, economically and technologically.

How do we respond to this change, and what makes us tick at work? Are we ruled by the work ethic, or liberated from the office through new technology?

In this dossier, we'll take a critical look at the world of work, and share some of the experiences of a variety of working men and women.

Features

1 Profiles:
Preferred roles at work

2 Too much work?
The overworked society

3 Women's work:
Equal or better?

4 What's your line?
Jobs and career moves

Getting started

In developing the Team Management Index, Charles Margerison and Dick McCann of Team Management Systems developed these four key areas at work:

① Read

② In pairs: tell how you are at home vs. how you are at work. different? give examples?

Extrovert	*Relationships*	Introvert
⟷		
Practical	*Information*	Creative
⟷		
Analytical	*Decisions*	Beliefs
⟷		
Structured	*Organization*	Flexible
⟷		

Do you think your behaviour at work differs from the way you behave at home – for example, are you more or less organized?

Preferred roles at work

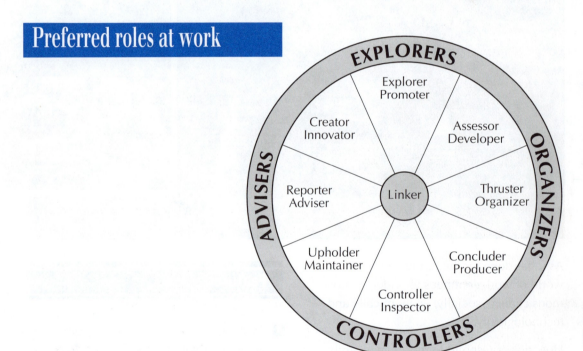

① Read.

Margerison and McCann went on to develop the Team Management Wheel in Australia. The Index (based on a 64-item questionnaire) has been used to produce work preference profiles on more than 200,000 managers worldwide. These profiles identify an individual's work preferences on the Team Management Wheel. As you read through the brief descriptions consider the team you work with.

① *Read.* + *Discuss* –

Reporter-Advisers	They are excellent at gathering information and putting it together in a comprehensible form. They are patient people who prefer to be sure they have all relevant information before taking any action. Others often accuse them of procrastination. They do not usually enjoy conflict and will move to defuse it or position themselves well away from any direct effects.
Creator-Innovators	They are 'future-oriented'; they enjoy thinking up new ideas. They are sometimes accused of having 'their head in the clouds'. They are usually not very structured and sometimes appear disorganized and absent-minded.
Explorer-Promotors	They enjoy being with people. They are advocates of change and are highly energized, active people who have several activities on the go at once. They are excellent at seeing the big picture but are not always interested in the details. They may sometimes 'get their fingers burnt' by pushing too far too quickly.
Assessor-Developers	They may not think up good ideas themselves but they are excellent at taking an idea and making it work in practice. They usually display a strong analytical approach and are at their best with several different possibilities to develop. They like organizing new activities but once these have been set up and shown to work, they will often lose interest.
Thruster-Organizers	This type enjoys making things happen. They will 'thrust' forward towards a goal, meeting conflict head-on if necessary. They excel at organizing people and systems to meet deadlines. They tend to be task-oriented and in their pursuit of goals may sometimes ignore people's feelings.
Concluder-Producers	These are strongly practical people who can be counted on to carry things through to the end. Their strength is in setting up plans and systems so that output can be achieved on a regular basis. For this reason they usually do not like rapid change. Their drive comes from a 'job well done'.
Controller-Inspectors	They have strong personal values and principles and these are of prime importance in decision-making. They usually have a high concern for people and will be very supportive of those who share the same ideals. Because of their strong principles, they will 'dig their heels in' when confronting opposition.
Upholder-Maintainers	They are more quiet, reflective people who enjoy the detailed side of work. They are usually careful and meticulous and can spend long periods of time on a particular task, working quietly on their own. They are comfortable working within established rules and regulations.

→ What type are you.

Discussion

- How useful do you think it would be to use such an instrument to put together an effective team?

- How valuable do you think these types of analyses are?

Word power

Match each role with the best three descriptions (from a-x) in the table below.

more concerned with practical results than with theories + principles

H.W.

Roles	Descriptions		
1. Reporter-Adviser	(a) analytical	(i) forceful	(q) realistic
2. Creator-Innovator	(b) methodical *systematic*	(j) pragmatic	(r) procedural
3. Explorer-Promotor	(c) principled	(k) unreliable	(s) stubborn
4. Assessor-Developer	**(d) cautious**	(l) reflective	(t) hard-headed
5. Thruster-Organizer	(e) original	(m) task-oriented	(u) entrepreneurial
6. Concluder-Producer	(f) law-abiding	(n) reliable	(v) dynamic
7. Controller-Inspector	(g) gregarious	(o) supportive	(w) absent-minded
8. Upholder-Maintainer	**(h) thorough**	**(p) low-profile**	(x) conservative

e k w
g, u, v
a i q
l m t
b n x
c o s
f l r.

very friendly, sociable
→ you 3 adjectives

Discussion

→ How would you describe people in the following jobs?

accountant	salesman	social worker
scientist	writer	self-made person

→ Do you think your descriptions are fair or are you stereotyping these professionals? If so, why?

WORD CHECK   1

procrastination   the habit of postponing action or decisions

to defuse   reduce the possibility of trouble

'head in the clouds'   unaware of reality

absent-minded   forgetful

advocate   supporter

on the go   running, happening

big picture   overview

'get their fingers burnt'   get hurt or rejected because they are too eager

head-on   facing, not avoiding

drive   motivation

'job well done'   satisfaction from completing a task well

prime   primary, principal

'dig their heels in'   refuse to move, be stubborn

photo copy - match, then ask questions

Getting started

- What's your working day like? Do you think you work too much?

must? necessary? just a reality? should change?

favorite least favorite day of the week.

?HW?

The overworked society

complain.

✓practise

Throughout the world, politicians, commentators and economists bewail the frustration, the waste of talents, and the poverty unemployment brings. But there is another side to this story which is only beginning to attract the attention it deserves: overemployment.

generally agreed

It is accepted wisdom that employer organizations are being revolutionized; large sections of their work are being contracted out, and the workforce pruned to a core elite.

cut back

Until now, attention has focused on the two most obvious victims of this process: the structurally unemployed and the expanding army of insecure self-employed. Employment problems are discussed in terms of lack of work; a new set of unemployment figures brings either good news – the jobless total down – or bad news, a fresh rise.

What has been omitted from the equation is there are no winners in this revolution. The core elite are as much victims as anyone else. In his book, *The Empty Raincoat*, Charles Handy sums it up in a useful but chilling equation: $\frac{1}{2} \times 2 \times 3$ = Production. Employ half as many people, work them twice as hard and they will produce three times as much.

■ ■ ■

Overemployment has become structural too. The upper echelons of the professions and industry probably spend more of their time earning their living than anyone since the factory workers of the early industrial revolution. However, this is not the most profitable way to exploit the skills and energy of the workforce. It is exhausting and stressful; the UK, which has the longest average weekly working hours in the European Union, loses a greater proportion of the working week because of illness than any other EU country bar one. Job stress is thought to cost the UK 10 per cent of GNP annually.

frightening.

The Guardian,
17th March 1994

Q

reaction

Read through this extract from a newspaper article and identify the three victim groups who have suffered from employment problems.

Discussion

after HW.

Explain Charles Handy's equation in your own words:

½ x 2 x 3 = production

Do you agree with this equation? If not, why not?

Word power

Find the right combination of the word parts below to complete the sentences about employment:

4 in pairs practice

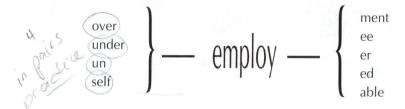

over
under
un
self

}— employ —{

ment
ee
er
ed
able

HW

1. The workforce is .... They spend half the day sitting around doing nothing.
2. I'm afraid he's .... He's got no qualifications, no experience and no motivation.
3. Most people used to think that being an .... was much more secure than being ....
4. .... is a relatively new phenomenon, brought on by companies reducing the number of .... to a bare minimum.
5. .... should think carefully before cutting their workforces.

Cultural connections

Language often reflects the culture of the speaker. This is particularly true when it incorporates value judgements. Discuss the questions raised by the examples given below.

Discussion excellent

Overworked?
How many hours a day would you consider reasonable?

Underemployed?
Is it better to keep people in employment rather than making them unemployed? What are the results of doing this?

Insecure?
If you are self-employed, do you feel insecure? What are the compensations?

Elite?
Who forms the elite in your country – the rich, the bureaucrats, some other group?

Do What questions do these questions raise!!

Poverty?
What sort of living standards would you consider to be 'below the poverty line'?

Role Play

NO!

Take on one of the following roles. Comment on your experience and your feelings about your status.

- an overworked employee
- an insecure self-employed person
- one of the long-term unemployed

check vocab ↓

WORD CHECK 2

to bewail complain about, lament

accepted wisdom generally agreed behaviour or position

to contract out give work to outside companies rather than use your own employees

to prune cut back, reduce

core essential, central

insecure not certain or permanent

structurally unemployed unemployed because that part of the economy no longer needs employees (as opposed to cyclically unemployed where jobs return after a recession)

to omit to leave out, not include

chilling frightening

echelon level, layer in society

to exploit use to one's own advantage

← personal information
← difficult topics
← scary movies

future E.U.

Getting started

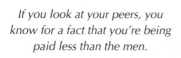

If you look at your peers, you know for a fact that you're being paid less than the men.

In this country, a woman has to be far better than a man to get promotion and a good salary.

You're wearing a skirt and they think, 'You're not the breadwinner.'

I couldn't even get an interview, so I changed my name from Stephanie to Steve.

What are the employment opportunities like for women in your country?

Equal or better?

Catherine Perry is a US business executive. In this interview she gives her views on women in the workplace, their problems and their strengths.

Listen to the interview and select those expressions which have the closest meaning to those given below.

Part 1
1. … and you are prepared to put in sufficient work to advance your career.
2. More and more of your time is taken up by the requirements of family and home.
3. Careers in business tend to take over a person's whole life.

Part 2
4. Many people are happiest in an office environment with lots of other people round them.
5. For women in certain situations, working from home can be a very good idea.

Part 3

6. Corporations not only do not help women with children; they actively make life difficult for them.
7. A lot of companies try to give excuses why this is so …
8. People should pay less attention to whether someone is male or female and more to the particular skills they bring to their job.

Discussion

Read →

In her interview, Catherine disagreed with a number of widely held beliefs about women in the workplace. Listen again to the interview and analyse exactly what her responses were to the following viewpoints:

not at the beginning

1. It is harder for women to get promotion in business than men.
2. It is normally men who make women's careers more difficult; women have fewer ego problems and are more supportive.
3. Freelance people usually prefer working at home. *some*
4. It is women who have to cope with the difficulties of working and having a family. *→ effect men too*
5. Women have special intuitive skills which make them superior to men in certain areas of the workplace. *No.*

Pairs
look at transcripts
p 164 –166
discuss + find
answers.

How far do you agree with Catherine's stated opinions?

have problems with someone
+ resent teachers leaving a mess in the room
–take your parking place
, what jobs.

WORD CHECK   3

resentment   bitter feelings
to make it   succeed in a career
opting out   deciding to leave, or quit
corporate politics   competition and
  rivalry within a company
corporate surrounding   office
  environment

(company)

freelance   independent, self-employed
tap into   make use of (a service)
to discriminate against   judge unfairly
to rationalize   explain with reasons
to lend itself to   be suitable for *room*
  –classroom
to bring to the party   *(slang)* contribute *–meeting room*
  to the group *– small club*
  – place to play cards.

why people what groups

–can be difficult
English class.
–to a teenager difficult
– piano lesson
– taking aerobics.
– dinner party.
→ rationalize taking English classes
→ Going in holidays
→ Not buying a

Getting started

I've worked all my life – left school at fourteen, went down the pit. I loved it. It's a tragedy, it is, closing down this pit.

I always wanted to be a nurse. Even as a child of ten or eleven, I knew this would be the job for me.

I seemed to have spent half my life studying. What for? That's what I want to know. There are no jobs for people like me.

Dread

2) Pairs
Interview

- What's your experience of work?
- Did you always know what you wanted to do?
- Have you had to change your job frequently?
- Have you found the job you really want to do?

Jobs and career moves

3)

Listen to the following people talking about their jobs and career moves. As you listen, complete the information for the table.

Interviewees	Job/profession	Current problems	Next step
François Bergerac			
Petra Telleman			
Carlos Rodrigues			
Matthew Tate			

4)

Discussion

- What's your line?
- Have you got a vocation?
- How long do you plan to stay in the same line of work, and why?

Getting it right

Phrasal verbs are common in informal spoken English. They are formed by combining a verb and an adverb or a preposition:

*And has the work **turned out** to be what you expected?*
*And what sort of job **are you after**?*
*… most companies **are cutting back on** research …*

H.W.

1) Sheet.

2) I ask question give examples.

3) Pairs they practice.
4) →(?)
H.W(?)

Complete the following sentences by inserting an appropriate adverb or preposition from this list:

about	after	along	around
away	back	down	forward
in	off	on	out
over	round	through	up

1. The new job turned .... much better than expected.
2. The company has cut .... on all areas of expenditure.
3. I'm afraid he's .... my job but he's not going to get it.
4. I had to turn .... the job despite the good salary.
5. They aren't taking .... any new recruits.
6. She had to stop work to look .... her children.
7. Don't worry. I'm sure something will turn ....
8. He gets .... really well with his boss.
9. It's never worth making it .... It's better to tell the truth.
10. I don't think this job is going to come .... It looks as if they're going to appoint someone internally.

H.W.

Word power

Try building up your word power by grouping common verbs with their associated adverbs/prepositions. For example:

to look – after, at, for, down, up …

1st *pairs!*

2nd as group
– show us act out practice

Try doing the same with these verbs:
to take – *away / in / over / back / after / off / along, / down / up / out / on / round /* *back / away) over* *around*
to turn – *away / in / over / back / round / down / on / through / up.*
to put – *away / in / off / down / out / up)*

Putting it all together

Write a letter of application for a job you would like. Include the following information:

* what you've done so far
* why you want the job
* why you think you would be suited for the job

* check some vocab.

WORD CHECK 4

to be into   *(colloq.)* be enthusiastic about, keen on

to turn out   finish, end

to be cut off   be removed from, distant from

to move into   change direction

mainstream   central

to look after   take care of

to be after   look for, want

tough   hard

to take on   appoint, recruit

afield   away

to start up   here, begin a new business

to go after   try to get

to cut back   reduce

'beggars can't be choosers'   when times are hard, you must take what you can get.

Postscript

'Work in the 21st century will be very different. We will all have to change jobs more frequently, accept periods of unemployment, and therefore no longer define ourselves by what we do.'

John Forsmann, Swedish industrialist

[Handwritten marginal notes: sports, art / music; book launch; camping? like being?; culture – pop music; politicis – generally accepted; beliefs; eating fast food is a mainstream belief; what other?; what do you want; – new job; – a way to have more time for art; learning English; afield – abroad; Would you go after; – a position in another city; – university country; position; drinking and driving – smoking]

4 Travel

The twentieth century has revolutionized travel. The car has given us the freedom to make our own travel plans. Air travel has shrunk the globe and put exotic locations on our doorsteps. Travel companies can now take us wherever we want to go – well, almost. And even today's few inaccessible spots will soon be handed to us on a plate: remoteness will be a thing of the past.

But what about the excitement of travel, the anticipation of new destinations? Haven't these feelings become dulled by our awesome ability to conquer the planet? Will travel soon be just another commodity to buy in the global supermarket?

In this dossier we'll be doing our own explorations into both the opportunities and the dangers posed by travel and tourism.

Features

1 Taking care:
Advice for travellers

2 Tourist Talk:
Signs to remember

3 Mixed blessings:
Tourism – for and against

4 A bad image:
'If only they'd stay at home'

39

etting started

Which of the following sayings describes your attitude to travel?

'Travel broadens the mind.'

Old saying

'I have recently been all around the world and have formed a very poor opinion of it.'

Sir Thomas Beecham, Bart., British conductor (1879-1961)

'Slow down, you move too fast.'

Paul Simon, American singer and composer (b.1942)

'A man should know something of his own country, too, before he goes abroad.'

Laurence Sterne, Irish-born British novelist (1713-1768)

'I dislike feeling at home when I am abroad.'

George Bernard Shaw, Anglo-Irish playwright (1856-1950)

'He who would travel happily, must travel light.'

Antoine de Saint-Exupéry, French aviator and writer (1900-1944)

i) Read talk about examples of travel experiences.

A question of style

1. Read the extracts on the page opposite. What mode of transport does each one refer to?

2. Extracts 1, 4 and 6 were written in the nineteenth century. Which features of style reflect their period and which phrases are different from modern English usage? Note your answers under these three headings:

   Vocabulary features   Structural features   Information

3. Now rewrite Extract 4 in a more modern style.

From The Traveller's Oracle by William Kitchiner, 1827

1

Advice for travellers

2

All passengers are requested to remain in their seats with their seat belts fastened until we have come to a complete standstill and the engines have been turned off. Please take special care when opening the overhead bins as items may have moved during the flight.

3

Always keep a special look out for cycles and motorcycles, particularly when overtaking or turning. Bear in mind that, owing to their size, two-wheelers are much less easy to see than larger vehicles and that their riders have the same rights of consideration as other road users and are more vulnerable. Drivers should leave plenty of room for pedal cyclists, in particular.

4

Of all species of fatigue, the back-breaking monotonous swing of this creature is worst; and, should the rider lose patience and administer a sharp cut with the whip that induces the creature into a trot, the torture can best be compared to the sensation of having your spine driven by a sledge-hammer from below, half a foot deeper into the skull.

From Life in Abyssinia by Mansfield Parkyns, 1853

5

Always take extra care when the weather is wet, foggy, windy or icy. Wear warm waterproof clothing – in bright, reflective colours, if possible. Ride slowly and brake early, as stopping distances can be doubled or tripled. Sudden braking could lead to skidding on hazards such as mud, gravel, snow, etc.

6

Never attempt to get in or out while it is moving, no matter how slowly. Never sit in any unusual place or posture. Remain in your place, without going out at all until you arrive at your destination. When this cannot be done, go out as seldom as possible.

From Travelling Past and Present, ed. Thomas A. Croal, 1877

Word power

Train, bus, car and bike can be classed as vehicles.

Which words from the extracts belong to the following classes?

✓ relations   bones
weather conditions   hazards/dangers

Here are some class words taken from the extracts. Can you think of some members of each class?

✓ creature   clothing
colour   two-wheeler

Getting it right

The following sentences from the extracts show different ways of expressing the relationship between **cause** and **effect**.

1) Read
2) Practice sheet
   (Pairs)
3) give
   HM

2. Please take special care when opening the overhead bins **as items may have moved** during the flight.
   (subordinate clause of cause introduced by **as, because** or **since**)

3. Sudden braking could **lead to** skidding on hazards such as mud, gravel, snow, etc.
   (verb phrase linking cause to effect)

5. 1. Bear in mind that, **owing to** their size, two-wheelers are much less easy to see.
   (phrase of cause introduced by **because of**, **due to**, **as a result of**, **on account of**, etc.)

4. **Therefore,** if I were you, I would certainly never go to bed.
   (sentence connector of cause introduced by **So, Consequently, As a result**)

Rewrite the following sentences using the construction indicated and making any other necessary changes.

1. Turbulent conditions in the air may cause items to move.
   (phrase of cause)
2. Take-off and landing are dangerous. Therefore, you must keep your seat belts fastened.
   (subordinate clause of cause)
3. Many road accidents happen because of a combination of bad weather and poor driving.
   (verb phrase linking cause to effect)

4. Never try to jump onto a moving train because you could easily slip and injure yourself. *(sentence connector of cause)*
5. Bad weather conditions have led to many delays throughout southeast Asia. *(phrase of cause)*

Now write four sentences of your own, using each of the constructions once.

Discussion

Which of the forms of transport described in the extracts do you consider:

the safest
the most dangerous
the quickest
the slowest
the most comfortable
the least comfortable
the most environmentally-friendly
the most environmentally-unfriendly

WORD CHECK   1

to shrink   make smaller

inaccessible   unreachable, usually referring to a place

spot   place

to dull   make less sensitive

awesome   wonderful, yet hard to believe

commodity   product

watery   here, at sea

standstill   stop

overhead bins   luggage racks in aeroplanes *(AmE: airplanes)*

species   type

cut   lash (of a whip)

whip   instrument usually consisting of a handle and flexible rod used to hit an animal to force it to go faster

trot   moderately fast running pace of a four-legged animal

sledge-hammer   large heavy hammer used for breaking stone

to skid   slip sideways on a road because the tyres fail to grip properly

gravel   loose stone forming the surface covering of a road

posture   position of the body

vulnerable   defenceless against injury

Getting started

1) Read +
  Discuss.

OR
2) Debate (2 Sided
  prepare.

*Every group of people needs a lingua franca –
even tourists. As English is the most widely spoken
and understood world language, it is only natural
that its use will increase. English will certainly
become the language of travel and tourism.*

*The English language is like a contagious
disease taking over the planet. Wherever
you go nowadays, you are constantly
confronted with English-language signs –
even in the remotest spots. Nowhere
seems safe from this virus.*

What can be said for and against these viewpoints?

Signs to remember

1) Read

2) Read +
  correct →

3) why funny.

Here is a collection of memorable signs written in English and
collected by travellers around the world. What makes each of them
funny? Can you rewrite them in a more suitable form?

Japanese hotel:
You are invited to take advantage of the chambermaid.

On the menu in a Swiss restaurant:
Our wines leave you nothing to hope for.

Outside a tailor's shop in Hong Kong:
Gentlemen may have a fit upstairs.

Outside a Swedish fur shop:
Fur coats made for ladies from their own skin.

Outside a tailor's shop in Nairobi:
Order your summer suit. Because is a big rush and we will execute
customers in strict rotation.

At a ticket office at Copenhagen airport:
We take your bags and send them in all directions.

In a Norwegian cocktail bar:
Ladies are requested not to have children in the bar.

At the zoo in Budapest

Outside a doctor's surgery in Beijing:
Specialist in women and other diseases.

At a hotel in Tokyo:
Is forbidden to steal hotel towels, please. If you are not person to do such thing please not to read this notice.

Discussion

(H.M.)

How would you give the following information in English to foreigners? Remember that your request should be precise and polite.

1. At a hotel: Quiet after 22.00.
2. Outside a tailor's: Made-to-measure suits in 24 hours.
3. At a roadside café: Own food and drink not allowed.
4. At a picnic site: Be tidy.
5. At a hotel: We charge for an extra day if you aren't out of your room by 10.00.

WORD CHECK 2

contagious   spreading uncontrollably
to confront   be faced with
virus   disease, corrupting influence
memorable   easy to remember
to take advantage of   gain benefit from something, exploit someone
chambermaid   woman who makes beds and does general cleaning in a hotel

fit   sudden illness which causes convulsions or unconsciousness, *also* violent burst of anger
fitting   trying-on of tailor-made clothes
to execute   carry out, put to death
rotation   succession, order
in strict rotation   one after another in strict order

Getting started

A holiday means different things for different people. Here are four holiday types:

(handwritten notes in margin)
① Pairs
  – destinations? World
  – type of people? attracted
  – type of tour / holiday journey?
  –
② favorite

Which holiday destinations do you associate with the above images?

Tourism: For and against

Another side of holiday travel is shown by the statistics in the chart below which illustrates earnings from tourism.

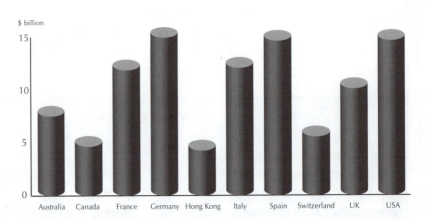

$ billion — Australia, Canada, France, Germany, Hong Kong, Italy, Spain, Switzerland, UK, USA

If tourism is such a powerful source of revenue, shouldn't everyone be in favour? Listen to the different views from a range of people affected by tourism. As you listen, complete a table for each of the five speakers under the following five headings:

Speaker   For tourism   Against tourism   Benefits   Drawbacks

Getting it right

Past

I used to

I am use to

The restaurateur said:

> Tourists **used to spend** a lot on meals and drinks.

Used to (with an unvoiced 's') can only be used (*used:* voiced 's') in the past tense, and is followed by the infinitive. It describes a habitual action or state in the past, which is not true now.

The restaurateur also said:

> **We are used to hearing** about street violence, breathing traffic fumes, and seeing rubbish.

Be used to (unvoiced 's') can be used in the past or present tenses, and is followed by a gerund. It implies that the person is accustomed to, or experienced in something; it is a normal pattern of behaviour.

Complete the following sentences with the correct form of **used to** or **be used to**; change the verb in brackets to the correct form, where necessary.

1. The British travel abroad a lot, so they *(drive)* on the right.
2. In the past visitors to our restaurant *(spend)* a lot more on food and drink than they do today.
3. People working in the catering business *(work)* long hours, even today.
4. As they lived on a very remote farm, they *(not see)* many people.
5. We expect that the number of visitors will increase; and many of those visitors *(receive)* a high level of personal service.
6. In the old days travellers *(have to put up with)* a lot of discomfort.

Now write six sentences of your own about travel and tourism. Write about how things used to be, what people used to do, and what people are used to doing now.

Discussion

Imagine that you have been asked to draft a discussion document about tourism in your area. In general terms, your document should represent a wide range of interests to both promote tourism and protect the community.

*   First, identify what tourist attractions should be promoted.
*   Discuss how to promote these, while at the same time protecting the rights of local people to enjoy their local environment.
*   Finally, draft your document.

A question of style

Handwritten margin notes:
1) Read →
2) 1st student attemp? loud for the whole class
3) in pair each person reads.

Contractions are common in informal speech and writing. In writing, the apostrophe is used to signal a contracted form.

Examples are:

didn't, can't, won't (negative particle)

he'll, we've, they'd (auxiliaries after pronoun subject)

we'd've, they'll've (compound contractions after pronoun subject: common in informal speech, but should not be written)

the company'd, tourists'll (auxiliaries after noun subject: common in informal speech, but should not be written)

Read out loud the following dialogue between a travel agent and a customer, using contractions.

CUSTOMER: We are looking for a holiday by the seaside.

AGENT: Do you have anywhere particular in mind?

CUSTOMER: We have never been to Greece. So that would be one possibility.

Handwritten margin notes:
what would: university'd like? wife'd like son'd like

AGENT: Just a minute and I will check our catalogues. Yes, here is one on the island of Corfu. Last week you would have paid double for this holiday. This week it is on special offer. Clients who have been there have been very pleased. The hotel accommodation is right on the beach. I do not think there are many places left. I will just check.

Handwritten margin notes:
→ 4) My questions:
what would you have done tonight if you hadn't come to english class - I'd've gone.
would you've gone ... ?

WORD CHECK   3

earnings income
revenue income
tremendously extremely
economical money-saving
   Note: economic means relating to
   the science of economics.
to tramp walk with a heavy step
picturesque pretty as a picture, often
   referring to architectural feature,
   for example, house, street, village
to draw here, attract

backwater isolated, secluded or
   backward place
backpacker person who carries their food
   and equipment on their back
impact influence
savage person belonging to a primitive
   society
be it whether it is
package combination of related elements,
   for example, travel services
45-odd about 45

Getting started

1) Read

2) Read head lines for vocab.

3) In Pairs :
invented the main points of the story.
- where - local reaction - result
- what happened? action taken

- 1 or 2 details.
4) Share with class!

Hooligans SMASH national monument

Holiday shoplifters arrested

My mugger was a ...... holidaymaker!

Lager louts *rampage* through holiday resort

What story do you imagine lies behind each of these headlines?

'If only they'd stay at home'

Q' warm-up. Have any of you seen/experience tourism getting out of hand?

tell us!

Read. →

Alistair Parker is the honorary Albion consul in the Alcoste, a popular seaside area in mainland Europe. In this interview he answers questions about the much-publicized behaviour of some of the holidaymakers from Albion – behaviour which has prompted the cry from Alcoste residents: 'If only they'd stay at home!'

Listen to the recording and complete the following sentences with words and phrases from the interview.

1) listen and fill in.

2) → audio scrip. vocab + more Q's

Part 1

1. It's blown up out of all proportion by ...., ...
2. Some get into brawls and this *creates bad image* for all the visitors here.
3. We must also show the local authorities that we're .... at home ....
4. We liaise with the local police to see that .... straight away.

1) fill in.

2) audio scrip vocab + Q's.

Part 2

5. There is a cost, but we consider it's ....
6. … nor as exporting it and ....
7. Oh, I see, so the people you send back home, they .... to be sent back home.
8. We feel we have a .... , here on the Alcoste.

Now vocab practice →

Word power

[handwritten: Read →]
[handwritten: "actually"]
[handwritten: → "really"]

Alistair began his first answer by saying:

*Well, **actually** it's a very **small** problem.*

The word 'actually' means 'in fact' and it qualifies or corrects an opinion. Now look at these sentences:

Do you think it's a good idea?

It's a really great idea.

The word 'really' intensifies an opinion. Both words are used frequently and almost unconsciously by many native English speakers. But they are not <u>interchangeable</u>.

Answer the following questions using the appropriate word – either **actually** or **really** – to suit the situation given in brackets. Pay attention to your intonation.

1. You bought a blue coat, didn't you? *(You bought a brown one.)*
2. You liked that Japanese film, didn't you? *(You thought it was excellent.)*
3. You haven't broken my vase, have you? *(You have!)*
4. That's an ugly building, isn't it? *(You think it's awful.)*

[handwritten: More questions :]
[handwritten: 1) Is the English class boring.]
[handwritten: 2) You have 3 children, don't you.]
[handwritten: 3) You think Belin is a relatively slow city, don't you,]
[handwritten: 4) Do you think we're having a nice summer so far.]
[handwritten: 5) You drive a porche, don't you?]

Putting it all together

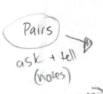

[handwritten: Pairs]
[handwritten: ask + tell (notes)]
[handwritten: group or pairs (?) practise asking Q's with new vocab]

In this dossier you've heard from a wide range of people involved in the travel and tourism industry.

Now you can carry out your own investigation by asking a number of different people for information about the following:

- how many days of holidays they take per year
- what types of holidays they prefer
- which countries/regions they enjoy visiting
- how they prefer to travel
- what type of accommodation they like to stay in

Finally, present and discuss the information you have collected.

WORD CHECK   4

lager   type of beer
lout   ill-behaved or misbehaving person
to rampage   rush wildly and destructively
hooligan   ill-behaved person
shoplifter   person who steals from shops
mugger   violent robber
skirmishes   spontaneous fight

brawls   (normally) fist fights
bona-fide   genuine
• **repatriated**   sent back to home country
to foot the bill   *(colloq.)* pay
hefty   here, big
draconian   very severe

[handwritten: more vocab]
[handwritten: small handful]
[handwritten: liaise (close cooperation)]
[handwritten: blowing up these stories]
[handwritten: blown out of proportion]
[handwritten: out of hand]

5 Education

Education is a process that every child goes through – whether born in upland New Guinea or midtown Manhattan. For some of us, school days are the best days of our lives; for others, they bring back rather different memories. Of course, education doesn't just mean the formal subjects that we learn during our days in school. In its widest sense, it transmits the values and accumulated knowledge of a society.

In this dossier we'll explore some crucial questions about the role of education in society today.

Features

1 School of life:
The learning experience

2 Dear editor:
Letter from a headmaster

3 Campus origins:
A comparative survey

4 A ne'er do well does well:
Is school worth it?

Getting started

Education arouses some very passionate emotions – some praising it, some condemning it. Here are some famous comments on the subject.

> ‘A civilized society must itself take responsibility for providing education. On the one hand, children must learn how to do things for themselves; on the other, they must learn how to help one another.’
>
> *Dr Maria Montessori (1870-1952), Italian educationist*

> ‘Education made us what we are.’
> *Claude-Adrien Helvétius (1715-71), French philosopher*

> ‘How do you explain school to a higher intelligence?’
> *Elliott in the film ET (1982), script by Melissa Mathison*

> ‘Indeed one of the ultimate advantages of an education is simply coming to the end of it.’
> *B. F. Skinner (1904-90), American psychologist*

How important has education been in your life?

The learning experience

Discussion

- What different educational experiences are suggested in the photos above and on the previous page?
- How appropriate do you think they are for the learner?
- How is education regarded in your culture? Is it generally considered as the key to unlocking new and exciting experiences; or is it seen as a trial to be endured?

Getting it right

Re-read the extract by Dr Maria Montessori on the previous page, and note the use of reflexive forms with **-self/selves**. We use these:

1. after verbs with the same subject and object
   He taught himself how to play the piano.
2. for emphasis
   A civilized society must itself take responsibility.
   A civilized society must take responsibility itself.
3. with **by** to indicate the agent alone
   They did it by themselves. (without anyone else's help)
   The form **on their own** can also mean 'without anyone else's help' or 'without anyone else's company'.
   We did it on our own. (no-one helped us)
   She lives on her own. (no-one lives with her)

We use the reciprocal pronouns **each other** and **one another** to combine two sentences:
   John taught Peter. Peter taught John.
   John and Peter taught each other.
We normally use **one another** where more than two are involved:
   All the children in the group helped one another.

Now complete the following sentences with an appropriate pronoun:

1. Since no one would help him with the exercise, he had to do it ....
2. Given the right environment, children are quite capable of learning ....
3. In a kindergarten or nursery school children are encouraged to play with ....
4. Twins are a very special case since they are often very supportive of ....
5. My brother and I supported .... during our university studies.
6. If you don't succeed, you will have only .... to blame.

WORD CHECK   1

to transmit   here, communicate from generation to generation

to accumulate   collect together in a mass

crucial   of critical importance

Getting started

- Do you think that students have too much freedom in school?
- Do you think that teachers should be strict or liberal?

Letter from a headmaster

On the opposite page is a letter written to a newspaper by British headmaster Paul Davidson. He argues that schools can best serve the interests of students if they are run on autocratic rather than on democratic lines.

As you read, answer the following questions:

1. What authority does a headmaster have in relation to teachers and students?
2. How can 'shifting the goalposts' create 'imbalance and confusion'?
3. What is the difference between a personal and an impersonal style of leadership?

Prepare a letter of reply to Paul Davidson giving your opinions for or against school democracy. You should include:

a greeting
an opening (this says why you are writing)
a main part (this gives your main message)
a conclusion
a closing

DEAR EDITOR

I have followed with concern the recent spate of letters to this newspaper advocating greater freedom in schools.

While not wishing to turn the clock back to the Victorian Age, I cannot agree with suggestions from certain quarters that students will benefit from a 'more democratic system'.

In short, a school is not and cannot be a democracy. The head is an autocrat, whether he likes it or not. In most schools, he has the power to hire and fire teachers as well as to admit and expel students.

Of course, there are checks and controls on this power, but with him lies ultimately the responsibility for all decisions.

On the question of discipline, I feel very strongly that wishy-washy liberal attitudes do not help the cause of teachers struggling to maintain a friendly but hardworking environment in the classroom.

Students respect authority (not tyrants). It is not a barrier to a good relationship but the basis on which it can flourish, enabling each side to get on with their respective tasks of teaching and learning.

Both sides know where they stand and where the limits are. To use a popular sporting analogy, shifting the goalposts creates imbalance and confusion.

Finally, a school is not like any other community. As a headmaster, I have to provide leadership for six hundred adolescents as well as fifty teachers.

The former are not willing to take part in government. The latter have the virtues and vices of a guerilla band: talented individually but unwilling to recognize the formal chain of command.

That is why I believe that a firm, autocratic style of leadership is what will work. But I would still call my style 'personal'.

I am more of a demagogue inviting personal contact than a statesman operating behind closed doors. I see no harm in this. Every leader must use the gifts he has.

Yours sincerely

PAUL DAVIDSON
M.Sc., M.Ed.

Word power

Opposites such as **hire** and **fire** and **admit** and **expel** are powerful literary and rhetorical tools. In each case they have the same syllable length and sound structure. So using them together can add emphasis to a text.

Now find the opposites of these words:

spate	(a) flood	(b) volume	(c) shortage	(d) answers
advocate	(a) request	(b) require	(c) discourage	(d) warn
benefit	(a) profit	(b) lose	(c) decrease	(d) disadvantage
flourish	(a) wither	(b) bloom	(c) survive	(d) increase

Here are some for you to do by yourselves:

democracy　liberal　confusion　former　virtues

A question of style

At the beginning of his letter Paul Davidson uses the phrase 'I cannot agree ...' which indicates strong disagreement. Using the right strength or emphasis is important in conveying the desired force of meaning. It is also an important feature of cultural style. In some cultures, expressing opinions forcefully and directly is valued; in others it is avoided.

You will now hear three short dialogues about discipline in school.

Indicate in the box opposite whether the speakers agree fully with each other (+), agree partially with each other (/) or disagree with each other (–).

1.
2.
3.

Now look at the phrases below. They indicate agreement, partial agreement and disagreement.

agreement	I totally agree with you / I totally accept that … I fully / completely agree. I'm in total agreement / I'm all in favour of that.
partial agreement	Up to a point / To a certain extent … I'd agree with you / I'd accept that, but ... You may have something there. / That may be so, but ... You could / may be right, but ... That may / might be right, but ...
disagreement	(I'm afraid) I can't / don't agree with you. (I'm afraid) I can't / don't accept that … I can't go along with you on that.

You are going to hear eight short extracts about educational topics. In each case the second speaker either agrees, partially agrees or disagrees with the first.

Write the number of the exchange in the appropriate box below. The first one has been done for you.

agreement	partial agreement	disagreement
		1

Sound advice

The main stressed syllable in a word is the syllable which carries extra force, e.g. bénefit, demócracy. But sometimes, the stressed syllable is different when the word appears in a different form, for example:

    bénefit   benefícial
    demócracy démocrat

Where are the main stressed syllables in the following words?

autocrat	autocracy	*authority*	authorize
responsible	responsibility	*recognize*	recognition
maintain	maintenance	*operate*	operation

Discussion

The subject for discussion is:

Education should focus on the skills needed for tomorrow, not knowledge about the past.

Remember to use an appropriate degree of forcefulness in your discussion, especially when agreeing and disagreeing.

WORD CHECK 2

autocratic authoritarian
democratic self-governing
spate flood
quarters areas
wishy-washy indecisive, vague
to flourish thrive, be successful
respective one's own

analogy comparison
virtue positive feature
vice negative feature
chain of command structure of communication of orders in an army which ensures that commands from the top are carried out

---

Democracy means 'rule (cracy) by the people (demo)'. What do the following words mean?
    aristocracy
    bureaucracy –
    plutocracy – rich
    technocracy – science

Getting started

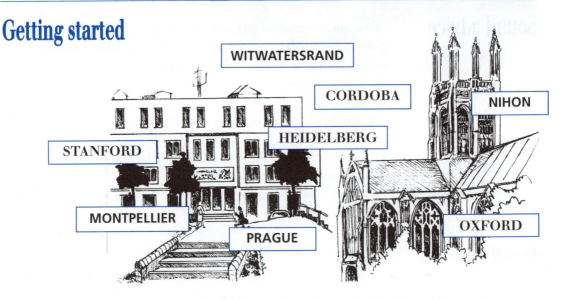

- Where are these universities and what do you know about them?
- What are the advantages of an ancient university, or an ultra-modern one?
- What is the purpose of a university education?

A comparative survey

Today you will be hearing from four students on an international work camp in the American state of Maryland. The students are Frank from the US, Manuel from Spain, Alberto from Italy and Brigitte from Germany. In this extract they are sharing information about the origins of universities in their countries.

As you listen, write down the information about the different universities.

Country	University	Founded	Other information
Spain			
Germany			
Italy			
United States			

A question of style

On the opposite page is a letter written to a newspaper by British headmaster Paul Davidson. He argues that schools can best serve the interests of students if they are run on autocratic rather than on democratic lines.

Suggestions involving the speaker	*Shall we* discuss this now? *Why don't we* postpone this till later? *Let's* start with this point. *I suggest* we write the notes immediately. *We should* finish in an hour. *We ought to* keep to the main points.
Suggestions to another person	*Why don't you* take notes? *I suggest you* start by giving us some dates. *(I think) you* should explain that a bit more. *How about* going round the table? *I (would) advise you* to spell all the names. *I (would) recommend* one of the Ivy League universities. *It's advisable to* read all the literature.
Reported suggestions	*She advised us* to exchange information first. *He recommended* that we (should) keep our report short. *She suggested* that we analyze the information.

Imagine you are a member of a team who has been asked to prepare a report about the best universities in your country.

1. Make six suggestions about how you should proceed.
   For example:
   Let's first list all the famous universities that we know.

2. Now make six suggestions, directed to the rest of the group, about how to organize the task.

3. Now reword six of your suggestions from 1 or 2 above as they would be reported by another member of the team.
   … advised / recommended / suggested ……………

Role Play

A foreign student wants to study or teach at a university in your country. What is your advice?

Sound advice

Spelling in English is notoriously difficult, because there is no one-for-one correspondence between a letter and a sound. For example, look at the spelling of these words while you read them out loud:

lau**gh** scar**f**   w**o**men w**i**nter   na**ti**on fa**sh**ion

Now look at these word pairs:

c**ough**	th**ough**
c**u**t	p**u**t
s**ew**	f**ew**

Can you think of other word pairs where spelling and pronunciation do not correspond?

Discussion

There are various programmes today which aim to foster international understanding. Exchange programmes give students an opportunity to see how those from other countries study and live; international camps bring together students of different nationalities.

- Do you think these initiatives are successful in promoting shared values and extending awareness? Or do you think that they simply reinforce national stereotypes?

WORD CHECK 3

to foster encourage
campus grounds and buildings of a
   university, college or school
to go round the table contribute one
   after another around the table
bound (to be) certain (to be)
legible readable
awesome here, enormous
enrollment registration
   Note: In British English verbs ending
   in 'll' often lose one 'l' in derivations.

enroll: enrollment *(AmE)*,
   enrolment *(BrE)*
install: installment *(AmE)*,
   instalment *(BrE)*
secular not controlled by the church
juridical legal
to leave to give on death, bequeath
estate here, possessions or property
sponsorship support

Getting started

Is education always the key to material success? Can you think of any examples which prove or disprove this point?

Is school worth it?

Colin Barrington is now the head of his own multinational company, but he openly admits that traditional education did nothing for him. His teachers called him a trouble-maker and a 'ne'er do well', but he went on to prove that a formal education is not essential to material success.

As you listen to Colin's interview, complete the table below in note form, selecting only the key points of his answers.

Part 1
  1. Early years   *One of eight children ...*
  2. Attitude to school
  3. Attitude to teachers
  4. When and how he left school

Part 2
  5. Early work experience
  6. What he sold
  7. How he started his first business
  8. His big break

Part 3
  9. How his success was received
 10. Plans for children; reasons
 11. Secret for success

A question of style

Colin described his career and expressed his opinions in everyday, colloquial language: 'a chance to earn *a few bob*', 'the city *hoity-toity* people' etc.

What other colloquial expressions do you know? When is it proper to use such expressions, and when should they be avoided?

Discussion

Do you have any sympathy with Colin's attitude to formal education? Is its only value to gain acceptance into a higher social class? Does education for education's sake have any value today?

Putting it all together

Use the following plan to prepare a project on attitudes towards education. You should try to get as wide a range of opinions as possible.

1. Design a questionnaire to collect attitudes towards education.

2. Collect the data from about ten people with differing educational experiences and backgrounds.

3. Prepare a report collating the results of your survey.

4. Present and discuss the results of your survey.

WORD CHECK   4

ne'er do well   (never do well) useless or lazy person

us blokes   *(BrE slang)* we boys/fellows

stall holder   owner of a market stall, kiosk

a few bob   *(BrE slang)* here, a small amount of money

gadgets   small, useful mechanical items

make the break   here, jump to great success

Eton   an expensive private school in England

city people   people working in London's financial centre – the City

hoity-toity   *(slang)* snobbish, upper class

Postscript

6 A Question of Sport

People's involvement with sport can tell us a lot about attitudes in any given society.

What do we count as sport: certainly, football, golf and tennis, but what about walking, fishing and riding?

Sport can be seen as a leisure activity, as an individual competitive endeavour, or as a collective team pursuit. It also highlights many potential conflict areas; between wealth and poverty, men and women, tradition and innovation.

In this dossier we'll examine some of these issues in sport.

Features

1 Sporty types:
Creating a legend

2 Sport for all?
Prejudices in sport

3 Pleasure and pain:
Fitness – a matter of opinion

4 Going for gold:
For love or money?

Getting started

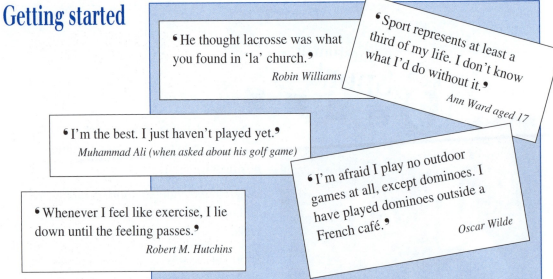

'He thought lacrosse was what you found in 'la' church.'
Robin Williams

'Sport represents at least a third of my life. I don't know what I'd do without it.'
Ann Ward aged 17

'I'm the best. I just haven't played yet.'
Muhammad Ali (when asked about his golf game)

'I'm afraid I play no outdoor games at all, except dominoes. I have played dominoes outside a French café.'
Oscar Wilde

'Whenever I feel like exercise, I lie down until the feeling passes.'
Robert M. Hutchins

- Which of these comments on sport best describes your own attitude to it?

Discussion

Read the magazine article on the opposite page.

- Do you agree that Ali was a sporting hero or was he just the product of public relations?
- Are there some sports you'd like to see banned? If so, why?
- Who are your sporting heroes? Why do you admire them?

Word power

The adjectives in the box below all describe personality.

- Find the closest equivalent (a-j) to each of the adjectives given.
- Suggest opposites for each of them.

1. dedicated	(a) relaxed	6. highly-strung	(f) keen
2. obsessed	(b) courteous	7. generous	(g) tough
3. enthusiastic	(c) self-assured	8. confident	(h) wound-up
4. easy-going	(d) unconcerned	9. gracious	(i) single-minded
5. competitive	(e) magnanimous	10. nonchalant	(j) fanatical

Take each of the words below and try to find as many variations as possible. For example: skill – *skilful, unskilled, highly-skilled*

talent   competence   training   build   fitness

Creating a legend

He could float like a butterfly and sting like a bee.

IN THE LATE SEVENTIES, Muhammad Ali was said to be the most famous person on the planet. His universal appeal never hinged on his boxing ability or any bland crowd-pleasing antics – it was merely testament to a greatness that no sporting icon has ever come close to. Ali caught the imagination of people of all ages and cultures because he struck a chord in the human spirit.

It wasn't until October 1975 that his career as a boxer assumed legendary proportions. Seven hundred million television viewers watched the 'thriller in Manila' – his bout against his arch enemy Joe Frazier in Manila's Philippine Coliseum.

The fight surpassed all expectations. Ali believed Joe Frazier was washed up, and started the fight by standing his ground and pummelling him. Frazier went down in the first round and was a pathetic figure by the third.

From oblivion, Frazier made a glorious return, hammering Ali in the fifth and sixth. By round 10 it was even and it was Ali's turn to call on astonishing reserves of stamina.

Despite brave protests from Frazier, his trainer would not let him return for the fifteenth round. For once Ali was not euphoric in victory. He was even gracious about Joe, saying the fight had been the closest thing to dying he could imagine.

Muhammad Ali was unique – dripping charm with his rapier wit, confidence, good looks and fun-loving nonchalance. Boxing remained a means to an end for him, not meaningful in itself.

WORD CHECK   1

to hinge on   depend on
bland   featureless, no character
antic   unusual or absurd action
testament   proof, evidence
icon   here, a venerated person
to strike a chord   be of significance
bout   here, match
arch   *(adj.)* chief, principal

washed up   *(idiom.)* finished, no longer a force
to pummel   punch quickly and frequently
to hammer   hit hard
euphoric   ecstatic
rapier   *(adj.)* very quick
nonchalance   lack of concern

Getting started

- What prevents people from participating in sport?
- Are there any sports which aren't open to you?

Prejudices in sport

 Listen to the extracts from four interviews. You will hear some contrasting attitudes towards sport. As you listen, complete this table.

Interviewees	What are they unhappy about?	What examples do they give?
Helen	....	....
Julie	....	....
Hamish	....	....
Mark	....	....

Word power

Listen to the four extracts again. For each extract note down the words or expressions which have the following meaning:

Extract 1.   *to retreat from something through fear*
               to be afraid of not succeeding

Extract 2.   *an area reserved for men*
               heroes to imitate

Extract 3.   *a great deal of money*
in all directions
protected areas

Extract 4.   *an obvious sign*

Now use one of the words or expressions to complete the following sentences.

1.   I can't afford it. It costs ....
2.   If you .... from this opportunity, you'll never get a job.
3.   She was shocked to find what a .... some sports clubs are.
4.   Golf courses are appearing ....

A question of style

The four speakers used a variety of techniques to make their points strongly and clearly. One key technique was to challenge their audience by using rhetorical questions. These are questions which do not expect an answer, either because the answer is self-evident, or because it is immediately supplied by the speaker, as shown in this example:

> *… what about the rest of them? They are deemed to be a failure at a young age as far as sports are concerned – so what happens? They lose confidence and get a sort of inferiority complex.*

Study the extract below. Incorporate three rhetorical questions at the points shown (?).

(?) Success in sport is at least 50 per cent due to your state of mind. Physical fitness, technique and strength all have their part to play, but the difference between winning and losing is often a matter of confidence.

(?) The importance of confidence can be seen in the growth of sports psychology as a new discipline. Top football clubs wheel in their own sports psychologist before an important game, top golfers retreat for a course of confidence-building after a run of defeats, and even amateur coaches put more and more emphasis on the psychology of winning.

Confidence is one side of the coin (?) . Fear is on the other side and you can see some teams try to instil fear in the hearts of their opponents.

Getting started

Why do or don't you play sport?

Read the extracts below. Then answer the questions.

1. What are the dangers of sports training at a young age?
2. What's wrong with intensive sports activity?
3. Explain why a 10 km walk might be healthier than a 5km run.

Fitness: a matter of opinion

Sport can seriously damage your health!

Excessive training and participation in sport at a young age can also be highlighted. Recent research has highlighted a number of serious risks bodies.

Young tennis stars were the pushed both mentally and physically led to very early ...

professional ... suffering from crippling pain ... placed on young muscles ... and bones developing. Pumping iron, ... muscle tone, working out — can do much more harm than good. Over-developed muscles turn to regularly exercised, ... weights can damage the spinal unnatural shapes.

DOCTOR COLLAPSES ON SQUASH COURT

... doctor ... from Melbourne Hospital, is in intensive ... severe heart attack ... Doctor Phillips ... was present at the City ... Sports Clubs which ... suffered the attack. A spokesman for the ... Phillips club said ... recently taken up sport and may ... had not appreciated what an intensive game ...

Daily Times
11th April 1993

Anyone for tennis?

As the length of the working ... increases, so sport may ... more and more intensive pursuit. A 5 km run rather than a 10 km country walk, 20 lengths rather ... , a multigym workout rather ... than a game of tennis.

Sport has its place ...

... ness meetings – but not ... ... place. Sport ... be done for pleasure not out of a sense of duty. Its benefi-cial effects on both mind and body need ... ... to take place over longer periods of time. In most cases ... bursts of intense physical activi...

Health Magazine, June 1993

Discussion

Discuss whether sport can damage your health.

Getting it right

The **gerund** (verb + **-ing**) is used to make the verb function as a noun.

In these examples, the gerund is the **subject** of the verb:

> ***Developing*** muscle tone, ***working*** out – call it what you like – it all can do much more harm than good.
>
> ***Lifting*** heavy weights can damage the spinal column.

In the following example the gerund is the **object** of the verb:

> Can you afford to risk **damaging** your health?

Certain verbs must be followed by the infinitive:

> Its beneficial effects need to be allowed **to take place** over longer periods of time.

Some verbs which take the gerund		Some verbs which take the infinitive		Some verbs which take both *	
dislike	practise	agree	promise	love	stop
miss	delay	intend	expect	remember	try
avoid	involve	allow	persuade	start	
enjoy	regret	manage	hope		
postpone	deny	decide	wish		
suggest	not mind				
consider	risk				
finish					

> * *Note:* Sometimes the meaning is different:
> *He is **trying to win** the race for the first time.* (= attempt)
> *Have you **tried walking** backwards?* (= experiment)

Rewrite these sentences by using a gerund to start each one.

1. It's difficult to start a business in this economic climate.
2. It's not so easy to think of a good example.
3. It's a bit late to call off the wedding now.

Complete these sentences with the right form of one of the verbs below:

take up	watch	windsurf	fight
throw	rest	retire	win

1. The boxer postponed .... his next bout until the summer.
2. You look exhausted. I would suggest .... for an hour.
3. He persuaded me .... badminton. I love it now.
4. We need to practise .... the ball as far as possible.
5. I remember .... my first race at this track.
6. Do you expect .... from the sport soon?
7. We managed .... the race on TV.
8. I'd like to try .... next time we're on holiday.

Discussion

Find out about your partner's attitude towards sport, using the following questions.

1. Do you enjoy sport?
2. Types of sport practised?
3. Years played?
4. Frequency?
5. Time given to sport each week?
6. In conclusion, what is your attitude towards sport?

 Now write a short report summarizing what you have found out.

WORD CHECK   3

excessive   too much

serious   not to be considered lightly

to hit the headlines   be in the news

beyond the limit   too far

professional circuit   series of professional sports events

crippling   disabling

stresses and strains   pressures on the body

pumping iron   (idiom.) weight-lifting

to work out   follow a routine of weight-lifting and other exercises in a gym

over-developed   too big

pursuit   activity

burst   sudden increase in activity

to appreciate   here, realize

Getting started

Michael Schumacher and Damon Hill, top Formula I racing drivers

- How much do you think a top racing driver is paid?
- How much are your top national sportsmen and women paid?

For love or money?

Christal Sheffield is a successful amateur sportsperson. Here she tells us about her sport and her attitude towards the division between amateur and professional.

Listen to her interview and correct the following statements:

Part 1

1. Powerlifting is the same as weightlifting.
2. In a squat, Christal lifts weights from the floor to above her head.
3. Powerlifting is her way of being both dainty and strong.

Part 2

4. Christal thinks it is unfortunate she is not paid for her sport.
5. She does not think it right that professionals in her sport are so well-paid.
6. She thinks most people take part in sports for self-satisfaction, like her.

Part 3

7. Christal does not think that athletes who have 'made it' should help newcomers, because they weren't given any help themselves.

Sound advice

*Christal in training
with powerlifting
weights*

Christal speaks with a strong southern US accent.

- Do you find that this obscures her meaning at any point? If so, where?
- If not, can you point to any phrases where Christal's style of delivery helps her meaning to be clearer, even though the words she uses may be unfamiliar to you?
- What conclusions can you draw from this about the importance of having 'correct' English pronunciation?

Discussion

Do you feel that increased professionalism is the only way to improve standards, to break records and to make a sport more entertaining? Or would you agree that professional athletes make themselves prisoners of the media and of advertising deals?

Putting it all together

We've looked at how factors such as personality, money and gender affect the way we experience sport. Prepare a short presentation on a sport you love or hate! Include the following:

Introduction: The sport of your choice, a brief description and your attitude towards it
1. Who plays it? Who watches it?
2. Where is it played?
3. How much does it cost? How much are players paid?
Conclusions: Future developments (e.g. amateur/professional)

WORD CHECK   4

to squat   here, crouch down with knees bent in approved position for powerlifting

toning exercises   physical exercises to improve muscles

tomboy   a girl who likes behaving like a boy

dainty   pretty and delicate

on a whim   on a sudden inclination, spur of the moment

ploughed back in   here, given back

meagre   very small amount
A difference can be seen in words ending in 're' *(BrE)* and 'er' *(AmE)*.
BrE: meagre, centre, theatre, metre
AmE: meager, center, theater, meter

astronomical (amount)   *(colloq.)* very large amount

Postscript

'Serious sport has nothing to do with fair play … It is war minus the shooting.'

George Orwell

'It may be the games are silly. But then, so are human beings.'

Robert Lynd

7 International Business

Today's world of business is becoming increasingly global. Decisions made in one country can affect distant financial centres within minutes. So what are the critical factors for success in this environment? Is it still a question of 'who you know', or is it the ability to handle the often stressful world of international deals?

The growing importance of global markets has had an impact in the worlds of sport and showbusiness. How are the big stars being used to promote products world wide?

In this dossier, we'll examine these aspects of today's international business as well as take a look at some rather unsavoury examples of big business practice.

Features

1 Roads to success:
   Is it who you know?

2 Rules of the game:
   Dealing internationally

3 Star approval:
   Dangerous liaisons

4 A question of honour?
   Big business and the moral maze

Getting started

- How did you get your current job?
- Which of the following were most important?

  experience   personal contacts

  qualifications   personality

Is it who you know?

 Listen to the extracts in which business people from different parts of the world talk about what they consider to be the key success factor. As you listen, complete the table below.

Extract	Nationality of speaker	Key factor(s)
1	Australian	*hard work*
2	Canadian	....
3	British	....
4	French	....

Discussion

- 'What you do should matter more than who you know.' Do you agree with this statement?

- How would you rank the following factors in business success?

  hard work   talent

  knowledge   communication skills

  leadership skills   motivation/drive

Getting it right

A common feature of spoken English is the use of modifying adverbs to strengthen or weaken an adjective or adverb.

*I now run it **completely** on my own.*
*It gives the country a **fairly** coherent industrial strategy.*
*We live in a **pretty** fair society.*

We can group these modifying adverbs as follows:

Neutral	Strong	Strongest
fairly	extremely	totally
reasonably	highly	completely
quite	very	fully
pretty		absolutely
moderately		entirely

Now use appropriate modifying adverbs from the list to complete the following conversation:

A: What did you think of his chances?

B: P............ good. He's got an e............ impressive c.v.

A: Well you'll be interested to know he didn't do v............ well in the interview. In fact he performed a............ terribly.

B: So, who got the job?

A: I don't think they've decided yet. It's between a woman from sales. She's q............ a bright spark. You know she's more h............ qualified than anybody else in the company. Somebody said she's got a PhD in philosophy.

B: And who's the other candidate?

A: He's an external candidate. Apparently he's a f............ fledged chartered accountant.

B: But I thought we needed a new sales manager?

A: Sure. He's also worked for a f............ long time in marketing overseas.

B: That sounds q............ useful.

A: Yes, it does. Anyway, they're going to be making a decision next week.

B: The sooner the better!

Cultural connections

Traditionally, employees have always been appraised by their bosses but in some companies, bottom-up performance appraisal has been introduced. Using this method, subordinates appraise the performance of their bosses.

*   How are you and your colleagues appraised at work?
*   Is there a formal system of evaluation and promotion?
*   Do you think bottom-up appraisal would work in your organization?
*   Do you think this performance appraisal system would work in all cultures?

WORD CHECK   1

break   opportunity, lucky chance

pile   stack of things put one on top of each other, here idiomatic; *heap* is also used

fitter   skilled, manual metal worker

to secure a deal   win business

ladder   *(idiom.)* career steps - see *pile*

go-getter   *(idiom.)* somebody who is very ambitious

coherent   holding together, making sense as a whole

Getting started

> ❊ ❊ ❊ **BUSINESS BEHAVIOUR** ❊ ❊ ❊
>
> ✓ Always shake hands when you first meet someone.
> ✗ Never talk business over the first lunch.
> ✓ Keep constant eye contact.
> ✓ Take time to get to know the people you are going to do business with.
> ✗ Don't talk about money until you have to.
> ✓ Speak your mind.
> ✗ Avoid personal criticism.

- In which countries do you think each statement might apply?
- What rules of doing business are followed in your country?

Dealing internationally

Alex Mott is marketing manager for Nokia mobile phones. As an American working in the UK for a Finnish company, he's in an ideal position to talk about conducting business internationally – and he also has some amusing reminiscences.

Listen to the recorded interview and complete the tasks below for each part of it.

Part 1
Select the phrases Alex uses which correspond to those below:
1. I do most of my work in the UK.
2. When I was in Eastern Europe, I used to work at a lower level.
3. It's not a good idea to antagonize people or to be aggressive.

Part 2
Answer the following questions:
4. What preparation does Alex recommend before going into a different culture?
5. What happened to Alex in Moscow? Tell the story in your own words.
6. What did he find amusing about the experience?

Part 3
Are these statements true or false? If they are false, correct them.
7. Alex says it is a good idea to set up two companies in new target markets.

8. He believes that gesticulation can help people understand what you mean.
9. In Eastern Europe he used to copy other people, so that they would see he was one of them.

Word power

Alex said 'your tone of voice … can put them off, and ruin deals …', meaning it can make people unsympathetic to you. To **put someone off** can also mean to distract them, while to **put something off** means to postpone it.

Use **put** + a suitable preposition to make sentences with the same meanings as the ones below. Choose from the following prepositions:

through   down   up   in   off   by

1. We can let you stay in our house until Thursday.
2. He's always saying how useless she is.
3. Hang on a moment, I'll connect you.
4. It's important to save some money for emergencies.
5. Stop talking! It's making me lose concentration.
6. I understand he's applied for promotion.

Discussion

- What problems might you expect in working or studying in a foreign country?
- How would you try to adapt to the culture of another region or nation?
- Do you agree with Alex that you have to adjust to the people of that country, and not expect them to adapt to you?

WORD CHECK 2

on the ground here, at a basic management level
hurdle obstacle
pushy aggressive
hitchhike obtain transport by begging for rides

gurney *(AmE)* light, portable bed for transporting sick or wounded people. *Note: (BrE and AmE)* stretcher
gesticulations conveying meaning by use of hand gestures
forward here, aggressive

Getting started

- How many of these logos do you recognize?
- How do companies manage to develop an international brand name?

Dangerous liaisons

CELEBRITIES can bring instant fame to a brand but they can also turn into a marketing nightmare.

Witness Pepsi's sudden withdrawal from sponsorship of popstar Michael Jackson's world concert tour in the early nineties. This followed accusations of addiction to pain-killers and child molestation.

Around the same time one of the world's top basketball players announced he was HIV positive and sportsgear endorsements were instantly halted.

Nevertheless the trend is towards increased use of big names, especially when advertisers are trying to reach young people. This is despite a whole series of potential pitfalls. There is the danger that the celebrity becomes the hero rather than the product, leading to consumers having no trouble remembering the star performance but difficulty in recalling the name of the brand.

Celebrities cannot be relied upon to always be the best ambassadors for the products they are meant to be endorsing. A supermodel was reported as saying she cleaned her boots with Bovril, a concentrated hot drink product which she was supposed to be advertising. A world-famous footballer denied ever using aftershave – least of all the brand he was promoting.

So what are advertisers looking for in a celebrity? They have to be clean, but not so squeaky clean to be boring. For the younger audiences, they have to have 'street credibility' and there has to be a connection between celebrity and brand. Unfortunately even the best possible fits can go wrong, as Pepsi would no doubt confirm.

Adapted from the Financial Times
18th November 1993

Read this newspaper article and answer the questions which follow.

1. Why did Pepsi withdraw sponsorship from the concert tour?
2. What is the consequence of the celebrity overshadowing the product?
3. What three attributes does a celebrity need to successfully endorse a product?

Word power

Find a synonym for each of the words below from the list (a-h).

1.	pitfall	(a)	vouch for
2.	witness	(b)	worthy of support
3.	sponsor	(c)	departure
4.	endorse	(d)	danger
5.	credible	(e)	match
6.	withdrawal	(f)	beyond reproach
7.	squeaky clean	(g)	support
8.	fit	(h)	for example

Vocabulary similar to the above is often used in politics as well as business. Use some of the words and expressions above to complete the following sentences:

1. He is a .... candidate for the presidency, partly because of his .... private life.
2. The sudden .... of the leading candidate from the election illustrates the .... of modern-day politics.
3. He had hoped for .... from many quarters. In fact he only persuaded one minister to .... his candidacy for the leadership.

Discussion

- Which celebrities are currently being used to endorse products in your country?
- Considering the very high fees paid to celebrities for this kind of work, do you find the endorsements convincing?
- Do you think the same celebrity can be used to promote a product throughout the world?

WORD CHECK   3

brand   a make or type of product bearing a trade-mark
nightmare   bad dream
addiction   complete dependence (on a drug)

molestation   interference with another person (especially sexually)
sportsgear   sports equipment
ambassador   representative
to wear out   exhaust

Getting started

- What is your initial reaction to international business and multi-national companies – do they suggest something exciting and attractive, or something negative and impersonal?
- Do you assume business people are generally honest?

Big business and the moral maze

The corruption scandals which shook Italy in the early nineties were perhaps the most publicised cases of bribery amongst senior executives, but they were certainly not the only ones. The so-called dirty tricks campaign waged by British Airways against its smaller rival Virgin Atlantic caused many British companies to adopt some kind of code of ethics.

At the same time in Spain the Filesa scandal involving the Banco Bilbao Vizcaya and allegedly corrupt dealings with the government led to a 12-page document dealing with confidentiality, conflicts of interest and related issues. Sweden took the problem seriously enough to have its own Institute against Corruption. Apparently, serious bribery involving thousands of kroner is unusual but Christmas gifts and business entertainment are perhaps becoming too lavish.

In Germany there was talk of a 'moral crisis' following the case of Jose Ignacio Lopez, lured away from General Motors by Volkswagen and accused of trying to poach former colleagues. It raised the question of where we draw the line between hard-headed business tactics and unethical behaviour.

The French, meanwhile, appear to be displaying their customary sang-froid. Every businessman knows what 'fausse facturation' means – inflating invoices with the extra going to line the pockets of national or local politicians who award contracts. However, none would agree that companies need to take any special measures against it. An official of Patronat (The Employers Federation) commented 'The idea of voluntary rules going beyond what is in the law is very Anglo-Saxon. We regard state control as sufficiently tough for companies not to have to make any special effort to sensitise their employees to it.'

*Adapted from the Financial Times
26th May 1993*

Read this newspaper article and answer the questions which follow.

1. What was the consequence of corruption scandals in Britain and Spain?
2. What 'corruption' may exist in Sweden, according to the article?
3. What was Mr Lopez accused of?
4. Why do the French feel special codes of conduct are not necessary, according to the article?

Discussion

- Where do you draw the line between acceptable and unacceptable business behaviour?
- How common do you think bribery and corruption are in your country?
- Do you think special codes of conduct are necessary?

Word power

The following words can all be used to describe business or business people. Choose the best synonym for each word from the three alternatives (a-c) given.

		(a)	(b)	(c)
1.	corrupt	(a) insincere	(b) immoral	(c) unethical
2.	hard-headed	(a) stupid	(b) ruthless	(c) unkind
3.	altruistic	(a) kind	(b) unselfish	(c) generous
4.	pragmatic	(a) down-to-earth	(b) thoughtful	(c) practical
5.	lax	(a) soft	(b) absent	(c) lenient
6.	competitive	(a) expensive	(b) tough	(c) winning
7.	ethical	(a) moral	(b) correct	(c) genuine
8.	self-interested	(a) ambitious	(b) ungenerous	(c) selfish

Now complete each of these sentences with one of the words above.

1. He argued that you couldn't afford to take .... considerations into account. Business was far too .... at the moment for such niceties.
2. He was accused of being .... , of having bribed government officials.
3. This was not a .... decision, it was purely .... ; we had to decide whether to invest now or later.
4. The company was accused of being very .... with its own rules and regulations. It appears that some .... employees had been selling their shares shortly before recent profit announcements.

Getting it right

Look at the use of the adverbs **too** and **enough** in the article:

*… takes the problem seriously **enough** …*
*… entertainment are perhaps becoming **too** lavish.*

1. **Too** comes before the adjective or adverb:
   *It's **too** soon to decide.*

2. The adverb **enough** comes after the adjective or adverb:
   *He didn't take the problem seriously **enough**.*

3. **Enough** is also used as a determiner – in this case it comes before the noun:
    There are **enough** profits for everybody to benefit.

4. **Too** and **enough** have related meanings. 'Too' means 'more than enough'.

Change the following sentences to use either **too** or **enough**. The first one has been done for you.

1. He was not tough enough.
    He was too easy-going.
2. She was too lenient with her staff.
3. He was too altruistic.
4. She was not pragmatic enough.
5. They were not ruthless enough.

Putting it all together

In this dossier we have looked at the following aspects of international business:

*   Qualities for success in business
*   Some cultural hints
*   Brand promotion
*   Business corruption

Write a summary of one of these aspects of business. Include your own experience and opinions.

WORD CHECK   4

to publicise   make public, announce in the press

dirty tricks   unethical behaviour

rival   competitor

to adopt   introduce, implement

alleged   asserted, but not proved

confidentiality   protecting the security of information

conflict of interest   presented with a choice where public and private interest conflict

bribery   act of offering money or gifts to achieve your objective

lavish   very generous

to lure away   attract in a devious way

to poach   steal

sang-froid   *(Fr.)* coolness, lack of panic

to line the pocket   bribe

8 Health

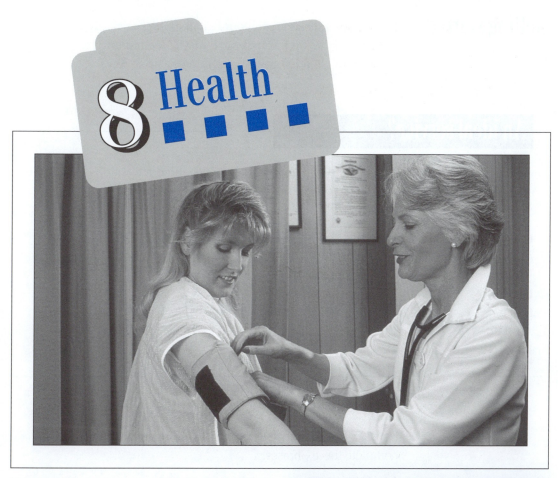

What are the key issues in health care today? Where resources are limited, doctors may be faced with some difficult choices. How do we assess the real needs of patients? Is health care a question of breaking new ground in hi-tech surgery, or providing more efficient preventive medicine against some of the widespread risks to health, such as smoking?

There is also the world of alternative medicine which today has become so much more widely accepted in many countries. What makes people choose this branch of medicine, and what role can it play?

In this dossier we'll discuss some of the key issues and controversies in the varied and changing world of health care.

Features

1 Health views:
   An ideal service?

2 Robodoc?
   Medicine in the 21st century

3 Health hazards:
   Tobacco – cash crop or killer?

4 Fringe benefits?
   Alternative medicine

Getting started

- Are you satisfied with your health care?
- Do you think it has improved during the last few years?
- How might it improve in the future?

An ideal service?

 As you listen to the views of patients and doctors from around the world, note down their major areas of concern, following the example.

Country	Patient/doctor	Area of concern
Canada	Patient	*too much hi-tech medicine, not enough low-tech primary care*
Ghana	Doctor	
Britain	Patient	
Australia	Doctor	
Italy	Patient	

Listen to the health views on the recording again in order to complete these phrases.

1. We can't .... endless money into health.
2. All the time we are advancing the .... of medicine.
3. We have made great .... in tackling diseases.
4. The problem is expectations .... resources.
5. Governments have to .... the costs.
6. There are no .... answers.
7. We all worry about our little aches and ....

Discussion

What type of health system do you have in your country?
What problems is it facing?

Word power

The diagram below illustrates the vocabulary you need in order to talk about problems.

to cause

to identify/spot

to face

to tackle

to solve

to avoid

to sidestep

PROBLEMS

trivial

serious

intractable

insoluble

People write letters about the most extraordinary problems. Use appropriate words from the diagram to complete the gaps.

A Mrs Swan wrote complaining of a problem she had recently .... with her neighbour – Mrs Kenton. This had started out as a seemingly .... problem of noise. She found that she was often woken at night by low-level vibration emanating from her neighbour's house.

She decided to .... the problem directly by speaking to her neighbour. Together they walked round the house trying to .... what was .... the problem. Following many unsuccessful attempts to .... the source of the problem, they decided to swap houses for one night.

The next morning, Mrs Swan emerged from her neighbour's house without having slept a wink. Mrs Kenton, on the other hand, had slept like a new-born baby. The two ladies had a much more .... problem to .... now. It appeared that Mrs Kenton's snoring had been the source of the noise all along.

WORD CHECK 1

to assess estimate

hi-tech/low-tech high/low technology

prevention stopping something from happening

preventive medicine methods designed to promote health and avoid sickness or disease

initiative new scheme or plan of action

pin-hole surgery surgery through minute opening

magnetic scanner machine used to look at nerve tissue in the body

two-tier two levels

swish (colloq. BrE) luxurious

to run down exhaust

Getting started

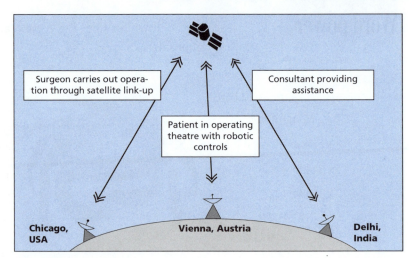

Surgeon carries out operation through satellite link-up

Consultant providing assistance

Patient in operating theatre with robotic controls

Surgery by satellite

Chicago, USA   Vienna, Austria   Delhi, India

What major breakthroughs in medicine do you think there might be in the next 20 years?

Medicine 2010

IN 1992 THE WORLD HEALTH ORGANIZATION (WHO) concluded that the world's population is not getting any healthier. People are reporting more frequent and longer-lasting episodes of serious and acute illnesses than they did 60 years ago. The world is still plagued by a string of nasty diseases, many of which afflict the growing elderly populations.

Scientists have been taking up the challenge by putting new technologies to use – telecommunications, computers, biotechnology and robotics are combining to transform health care. Here is some idea of what may be to come.

We can expect drugs for hitherto untreatable diseases. There will be easy-to-use medical tests that predict a person's prospective state of health throughout his lifetime so that steps can be taken to prevent diseases. There are certain to be surgical robots operating with a precision that puts their human counterparts to shame. Doctors, nurses, hospitals and manufacturers will all be linked through a network of computers, telephones, optical fibres and satellite link-ups that patients can plug into.

Perhaps most exciting are the advances being made in genetic engineering. It is reckoned that by 2010 gene doctors will have found a way of dealing with most diseases caused by single gene defects. Over the next 50 years most common diseases should have succumbed to gene therapy. More controversially, gene doctors also want to shape human destiny. Gene therapy could be developed to correct genetic defects and so eradicate disease passed down from one generation to another. It could also enhance or improve "good" traits – for instance an extra copy of the human growth-hormone gene could be added to increase height. In this way medicine will have moved from the business of curing or caring into the more ethically dubious areas of life enhancement and eugenics.

The Economist, 19th March 1994

When you have read the article, answer these questions:

1. Which part of the population is most afflicted by disease?
2. Will robotic surgery be more precise than human surgery?
3. What aspect of genetic engineering is considered controversial?

Discussion

- What do you think about genetic engineering?
- Do the benefits outweigh the risks?
- Would you be happy to engineer 'life' so genetic diseases were eradicated?

Getting it right

There is a large range of constructions which can be used to express different degrees of **probability.** For example:

> *Over the next 50 years most common diseases **should** have succumbed to gene therapy.*

> *It **could** also enhance or improve 'good' traits.*

We can represent the degree of probability according to the following scale:

Certainty   I'm *(absolutely) sure* that a cure will be found.
                              certain
                              positive
A cure will *definitely/certainly* be found.
A cure is *certain* to be found.
                   sure
                   bound

Probability   It's *(very) likely/probable* that a cure will be found.
A cure is *(quite) likely* to be found.
A cure *should* be found.

Possibility   A cure *may* be found.
                   could
                   might

Improbability   It's *(very/highly) unlikely* that a cure will be found.
                              improbable
A cure is *unlikely* to be found.

Impossibility   I'm *sure* that a cure won't be found.
                   certain
                   positive
A cure *definitely/certainly* won't be found.
A cure *can't (possibly)* be found.

Complete the sentences with an appropriate expression.

1. Robotic surgery is .... to be introduced sooner or later. *(certainty)*
2. Medical information such as patient records .... be sent down the line using a modem. *(possibility)*
3. It's .... some single-gene diseases .... be curable by the end of the century. *(probability)*
4. A cancer cure .... be found before the end of the century. *(improbable)*
5. Multi-gene diseases such as heart disease .... be cured for some time. *(impossible)*
6. It's .... that a cure for AIDS .... be found for some years. *(improbable)*
7. Scientists .... identify the gene responsible for multiple sclerosis in the near future. *(possibility)*
8. We .... be able to use telemedicine to reduce health costs soon. *(probability)*

Cultural connections

Drug-prescribing practices vary enormously from country to country. For example in France, lots of cholesterol-lowering drugs are prescribed. In the UK they are hardly heard of. In the US, drugs to reduce hypertension are widely administered, in other countries much less so. Levels of disease also vary enormously; for example, the level of heart disease in Glasgow, Scotland is ten times higher than in Spain.

- What factors do you think account for these differences?
- What medical complaints are most common in your country?

WORD CHECK   2

acute   intense, severe
to plague   afflict (with disease or hardship)
string   a lot of
nasty   unpleasant
to afflict   trouble, cause to suffer
burden   weight
to explode   increase dramatically
to take its toll   cause damage/suffering
hitherto   previously

link-up   connection
to succumb   give in to
to shape   influence
to eradicate   remove, get rid of
to enhance   improve
trait   characteristic
eugenics   science of influencing hereditary qualities of a race

Getting started

- How would you classify a cigarette – as a drug, a poison, a mildly-dangerous substance, or a pleasure?
- Do you think cigarette smoking is on the decline in your country? If so, why?

Tobacco: cash crop or killer?

FOR DECADES NOW, cigarette smoking has been on the decline in North America, Western Europe and Australasia but during this same time there has been considerable growth in China and Asia. As fast as smokers are giving up in the developed world, they are taking it up in the developing world.

It seems that smoking is closely connected with a nation's sense of liberty. Following the collapse of communism in Eastern Europe, the number of smokers rocketed to nearly 40 per cent of the population. This part of the world represents a potentially lucrative market for the tobacco multinationals – they have already invested millions of dollars in a market which is 40 per cent bigger than the US.

However it pales into insignificance when you look at the world's largest market, China. There are already 300 million smokers and the country has almost limitless potential.

From the Chinese health authority's point of view, these figures represent a health disaster in the making. In twenty to thirty years, they calculate that on the basis of current trends, 2 to 3 million smoking-related deaths per year will occur.

Reversing these trends is going to be an uphill struggle. In some developing countries like Malawi, tobacco is the cash crop; in others such as India, tobacco has been chewed rather than smoked for centuries.

As can be seen in countries where smoking has finally started to decline, it takes a major shift in social attitudes to change smoking habits. Smoking has to be seen as hazardous, abnormal and socially unacceptable behaviour.

Unfortunately, in most of the developing world, it is currently associated with the trappings of the good life – fast cars, beautiful people and a wealthy and liberated life style.

Read the article and then answer these questions:

1. What is the connection between the collapse of communism and the increase in smoking?
2. Why is it going to be so difficult to reverse the current trends in the developing world?

Word power

The language of trends can be expressed in different ways:

… there has been considerable growth in China and Asia.

… the number of smokers rocketed …

… smoking has finally started to decline …

Upward trends		Downward trends		Static trends	
Verbs	*Nouns*	*Verbs*	*Nouns*	*Verbs*	*Nouns*
to increase	an increase	to decrease	a decrease	to remain stable	stability
to rise	a rise	to decline	a decline	to stagnate	stagnation
to grow	growth	to fall	a fall	to flatten out	–
to climb		to drop	a drop	to plateau	a plateau
to rocket		to plummet			
to spiral					

Use words from the table above to complete the following passage about health care trends.

Demographic changes underlie many of the problems national health care systems will face in the 21st century. In the developed world the number of older people has been on the i.............. for many years. This change in the demographic structure has been caused by a marked d.............. in the birth rate. As the population g.............. older, the rate of disease r.............. . In addition, the demands for more sophisticated health care has r.............. over the last 20 years. While it is true that the rate of contagious diseases has p.............. , the rate of serious congenital conditions such as heart disease have g.............. . Of course, one of the 'problems' is that diagnostic tools have improved greatly, often leaving us in no doubt what we are suffering from. Perhaps the only way to control s.............. health costs is to reduce expectations. However, for the moment there is no sign that health care costs are f.............. out, let alone d.............. .

Discussion

Do you think smoking should be banned in all public places? What are the arguments for and against?

WORD CHECK   3

decade ten years

to give up stop (a habit)

to take up start (a habit)

lucrative profitable

to pale into insignificance to become so small that it is hardly noticed

in the making about to happen

uphill struggle difficult problem to solve

cash crop agricultural crop grown to raise money

adept skilled

abnormal not normal

trappings accessories

Getting started

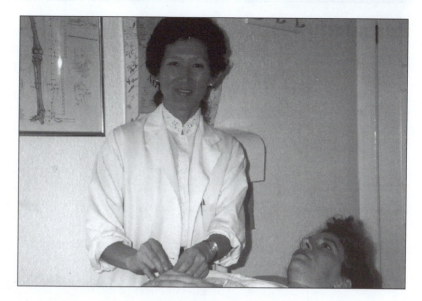

*Dr Lily Kyan prepares a
patient for acupuncture
in her London clinic*

- Have you ever visited an acupuncturist?
- What about a homeopath or a chiropractor?
- What's your view of alternative medicine?

An alternative view

Dr Lily Kyan is a medical practitioner from China, who has been trained in both western and alternative medical techniques. In this interview she discusses the uses of acupuncture and related treatments, and the attitudes of some western doctors towards them.

Listen to the interview and answer the following questions.

Part 1

1. What is Lily's medical background and experience?
2. What are the main fields she is currently working in?
3. How does she classify aromatherapy?
4. What sort of materials are used in Chinese herbal medicine?

Part 2

5. What sort of people use alternative medicine?
6. What sort of ailments does Lily treat?

Part 3

7. Does alternative medicine have the same status as western medicine?
8. What does Lily wish western doctors would do with regard to acupuncture?

93

Sound advice

Lily combines some of the features of her own native language with a natural use of English idioms; for example, 'but having said that', 'to a certain degree' and 'some of them can be very severe!'

- Do you think her meaning is unclear at any point? If so where? What causes this?
- How important do you think it is to be 100 per cent accurate when speaking a foreign language?
- When you are speaking English, do you try to become as much like native speakers as you can, or are you more concerned to express your own personality through the language?

Putting it all together

Study the statements below and prepare one of them as a topic for discussion in class:

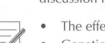

- The effectiveness of alternative medicine is all in the mind.
- Genetic engineering is taking medical science in the wrong direction.
- Health care cuts are inevitable for all countries.

WORD CHECK   4

rehabilitation medicine   branch of medicine which deals with restoring patients to a normal life

aromatherapy   using oils from aromatic plants to improve health

to itch   have an irritating sentation (which necessitates scratching)

side-effects   secondary (often undesirable) results of treatment

practice   here, professional work of a doctor

hocus-pocus   tricks of a conjurer or showman

Postscript

50%

of all illness in the developed world is caused by stress.
Japanese doctor

of all my patients come to see me because they haven't anybody else to talk to.
British general practitioner

of the drugs on the market are completely useless – pure placebos.
French pharmacologist

9 The Media

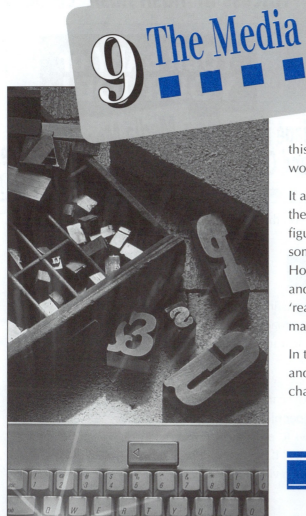

Words and images from the ever-expanding world of the media touch all our lives – and in years to come this industry is likely to be the western world's biggest employer.

It also raises numerous areas of debate. Does the drive for increased circulation or viewing figures justify sensational reporting – or as some would call it – scandalmongering? How far is the use of bad language on TV and in the press justified by the portrayal of 'real life'? To what degree are our opinions manipulated by the media?

In this dossier we'll examine these issues, and discuss how media technology is changing our world for the future.

Features

1 What scandal?
Creating a scandal

2 Language limits:
Expletives deleted

3 Form and substance:
Image maker

4 A changed world?
Communacopia

Getting started

Princess in 'hush hush' clinic trip

'Now I'm set for love' says tennis star

YOUR BABY or YOUR JOB!

Twelve ex-lovers to sue President

'Our marriage is OK' say Dick and Cindy

Media Mogul's Mistress bares ALL

What stories do you think lie behind these headlines?

Creating a scandal

Listen to the extracts in which six different people give their views on the media's approach to scandal. As you listen, note down each person's attitude towards scandal stories.

Discussion

- What makes a scandal in your country's media and how seriously do people take scandals?
- Are there laws to protect the private individual from the media in your country? If not, should there be?
- What's your own view on sensational reporting in the newspapers?

A question of style

The way you express your opinions depends on how strongly you feel, and your preferred style:

Strong	I'm convinced we should … I'm sure … There's no doubt that …
Moderate	In my opinion, … As far as I'm concerned, … I feel we should …
Weak	Maybe we could consider … We might think about …

Listen to the recording. Classify the opinions (1-8) you hear as: strong (s) moderate (m) weak (w).

1.   5.
2.   6.
3.   7.
4.   8.

The strength of your opinion can also be modified by the adjectives, you choose to use. Classify the negative adjectives in the box below under these three headings: **Strong Moderate Weak**

disgraceful	appalling	disappointing
poor	adequate	satisfactory
acceptable	dreadful	dull
mediocre	tedious	scandalous

Now use these adjectives to express your opinions about the following:

- a TV programme you've seen recently
- a newspaper you never buy
- a place you try to avoid

WORD CHECK 1

scandalmongering spreading malicious gossip

fuss the treatment of unimportant matters as important

second-rate inferior, poor quality

sordid distasteful, coarse, ignoble

to deserve be worthy of, earn

to get up to do something, usually against the rules

muck-raking digging up sensational stories about somebody's past

to hound chase, pursue without consideration

tabloid newspaper which appears in small/half size (cf. broadsheet), it also means a mass-circulation popular newspaper

to pick on select unfairly for criticism or abuse

to splash print all over

voyeuristic obtaining pleasure by observing the private (usually sexual) lives of others

to undo reverse, change back to original state

indiscretion action which is unwise, not discreet

to backfire come back against yourself

Getting started

'Just because you hear bad language on the TV doesn't mean you're going to use it or in some way become corrupted.'
Dana Rickson, aged 19

'I can't stand bad language on the TV. It's no wonder children swear so much.'
Susan Charman, mother of three

'I just get embarrassed for my parents. Bad language doesn't bother me.'
Gianni Petrocelli, aged 16

- How much bad language do you hear on the radio or on TV ?
- How do you feel about it?
- Are things becoming more relaxed?
- Where would you draw the line between what is acceptable and what is not?

Read this report and answer the questions which follow.

Expletives deleted

SOME PEOPLE violently object to the use of swear words on television and in films. For those who object, it is an extremely emotive subject; it is even seen as a symptom of the decline in moral values. Others cannot see what all the fuss is about – just because you are exposed to bad language does not mean your own sense of judgement should be affected.

In Britain, many swear words have now become acceptable – for example 'blast' and 'damn' are now almost universally seen as part of everyday language and therefore cause no offence when broadcast. The boundaries of acceptability have shifted particularly in the case of blasphemous swear words. Bill Bryson points out in his book *Mother Tongue* that before 1870, 'God damn', 'Jesus' and even 'Hell' were far worse than the extreme scatological and sexual swear-words which cause most

THE LANGUAGE ON THIS SHOW IS ✳✳!✳✳!! TERRIBLE !

offence nowadays. He adds, 'no other language approaches English for the number of delicate expletives of the sort you could safely say in front of your maiden aunt: darn, drat, gosh, golly, goodness gracious, jeepers, shucks and so on.'

On the other side of the Atlantic, the Rating Code Office of Hollywood has a list of seventeen words which will earn a film a mandatory R-rating. In fact, as Bill Bryson comments, 'swearing seems to have some near universal qualities. In almost all cultures, swearing involves one or more of the following: filth, the forbidden, and the sacred, and usually all three.'

On the subject of swearing and the media he goes on to note: 'Most of the quality newspapers in Britain have freely admitted expletives to their pages when the circum- stances were deemed to warrant it ... ironi- cally the tabloid newspapers, though usually specializing in matters of sex and prurience, are far more skittish when it comes to printing swear words.'

A recent study into broadcast language reached three clear conclusions: first, people believe that this is a complex area and there is no laundry list that should be banned; second, they think giving offence should be avoided, and third, they feel strongly that the scene and context must justify the use of bad language.

1. What are the three categories of swear words mentioned?
2. What do you think is meant by an R-rated film?
3. What difference between tabloid and quality press editorial policy is noted?

Discussion

Do you agree with these conclusions about the use of bad language in the media?

- It is a complex area and no clear-cut blacklist can be drawn up.
- The media should avoid offending their viewers and readers.
- It must be justified by the scene and context.

Word power

Most of the words below are used in the report. Match synonyms or equivalents in the context of the article from the two lists.

1.	swear word	(a)	judge
2.	scatological	(b)	nervous
3.	blasphemous	(c)	popular
4.	quality press	(d)	expletive
5.	tabloid	(e)	justify
6.	laundry list	(f)	profane
7.	deem	(g)	filthy
8.	prurience	(h)	serious papers
9.	skittish	(i)	lasciviousness
10.	warrant	(j)	long list of items

Now use words from the lists on the previous page to complete these sentences.

1. The .... press are .... about running sensational scandal stories as they do not want to be accused of ....
2. The film last night did not .... the use of .... I found it very offensive.
3. The censors obviously .... the programme to be .... But surprisingly the church said they felt the .... were very mild.

Cultural connections

National terms of abuse vary enormously. Below are some of the worst insults in different parts of the world (translated into English!)

China:	turtle
Norway:	devil
France:	cow
Xhosa, South Africa:	your mother's ears

On the other hand, the Japanese, Malaysians and most Polynesians have no native swear words at all.

• What types of words are considered abusive in your language?
• Are you familiar with any offensive English words?

WORD CHECK 2

fuss trouble
to shift change
scatological obscene, especially concerning excretion
blasphemous speaking abusively about something sacred
mandatory obligatory
R-rating restricted for viewing
filth here, dirty, obscene language

sacred deserving respect, something holy
expletive swear word
to deem consider
to warrant provide reason for
prurience unhealthy interest in sexual matters
skittish shy, unsure
laundry list long list of words or items
to ban forbid, prohibit

Getting started

Why do you think some people come over better on television than others?

Image maker

Meryl Griffiths is a communications consultant who has worked with a variety of public figures, including politicians, preparing them for appearances on TV or radio.

Listen carefully to the points she makes, and correct the inaccuracies in the following notes on her interview.

Part 1
1. Meryl has to get rid of her clients' bad habits and replace them with new ones.
2. There is no such thing as a 'natural' on TV.

Part 2
3. People under pressure forget their normal behaviour and do irrational things.
4. The leading politician she worked with had a woolly intellect and couldn't remember what he was saying.

Part 3

5. A politician should not wear an expensive suit if he's working with poor people.

6. When we make judgements about politicians' credibility, we make them mostly on their visual impression, and not on their style of delivery or the words themselves.

7. A politician who wants to get across a difficult message has to be assertive and confident.

8. Journalists and politicians conspire to keep messages clear and simple, because they know that the public is too lazy to complain and will not challenge well-packaged reports.

Role Play

Role 1:

You are a journalist. Interview your partner, an experienced politician. Seek responses to the following statements:

*   The media has cheapened politics.
*   What you look like is more important than what you say.
*   How you say it is more important than what you say.
*   Anybody with money and looks can make it to the top.

Role 2:

You are an experienced politician. Give your opinions in answer to the journalist's questions.

WORD CHECK   3

to come across   here, communicate

to harangue   make a loud and aggressive speech

approbation   approval

to dilute   weaken

to mumble   speak indistinctly

vulnerable bits   here, private parts of the body

concrete   here, specific

woolly intellect   unclear mind

to pitch up   here, bring the voice up

cut and dried   *(colloq.)* definite

aspirational   in a manner to excite hope

empathy   feeling the same as

deflected   turned aside

sound bites   small, easily digested portions of sound recordings

potted version   condensed and easy to understand

in-depth   deep, thorough

reinforcement   here, strengthening of existing idea(s)

Getting started

The television satellite shown here links a remote Indian village in Gujarat with the the country's major centres and the rest of the world.

- What effects do you think such links have on the lives of ordinary people?
- Do you feel your world has got smaller as technology has developed?
- What changes in media and related technologies do you forecast for the 21st century?

Communacopia

LARGE INTERNATIONAL corporate forces taking advantage of rapid technological change are gathering. These forces are likely to transform the media business over the remaining years of this century and equally transform the level of choice available, at least in theory, to consumers.

Politicians glibly revive old visions of creating 'superhighways' of limitless capacity down fibre optic strands as thin as human hair, usually without going into the specifics of how it is going to happen and who is going to pay. However, ten years after the first wave of such talk, this time there is some reality to the vision.

Goldman Sachs last year predicted 'a true revolution in the delivery of entertainment, information, transactional and telecommunications service may be at hand'. This marrying of technologies will create the new world of 'Communacopia'.

Of course, people will still read a general newspaper or magazine and watch a mainstream television channel in order to be surprised, amused, come across something they did not know they wanted to know, or share in the feeling of being part of a larger society or culture.

Yet, increasingly, there will be a growing tier of personal print and visual media as well as computers programmed to hunt databases and to assemble specific packages of information to match the taste and needs of individual consumers.

Rupert Murdoch, Chairman of the News Corporation, recently talked about five major industries – computers, telecommunications, television, entertainment and publishing converging into a single giant industry.

As Mr Murdoch embarks on a new phase of his bid for worldwide media domination, he did not persuade everybody with his further claim that technology was undermining the power of the media mogul by greatly increasing the number of competing choices available to the consumer.

Adapted from the Financial Times, 6th October 1993

Read this extract from a newspaper survey on changes in the media industry. Then answer the questions on the next page.

1. What example of a large corporate force does the survey give?
2. Why is there some doubt whether the level of consumer choice is going to increase?
3. How would you define superhighways and communacopia?
4. What will the two broad types of media be in the future?

Discussion

- What visual and print media do you regularly come across?
- Would you like to see or be able to access more?
- Do you think the merging of technologies is going to give the consumer a greater and better choice of news, entertainment and information?

Getting it right

The power of language to communicate messages successfully is greatly helped by the use of linking words:

… usually without going into the specifics of how it is going to happen and who is going to pay. **However,** *ten years after the first wave of such talk, this time …*

Yet, *increasingly, there will be a growing tier of personal print and visual media* **as well as** *computers which will be programmed to hunt …*

1. Linking words which signal logical relationships

Cause *therefore, so, consequently, hence (formal), thus (formal), because of this, that's why*	Industries are converging. *Therefore* there will be less competition, and consequently choice, in the market.
Reason *as, because, since*	*Because* subsidies have been removed or reduced, commercial TV now dominates the small screen.
Contrast *yet, however, nevertheless, still, but, even so, all the same (informal)*	The media moguls aim to dominate the market. *However,* there are still lots of independent companies.
Contradiction *in fact, actually, as a matter of fact*	You would imagine we all watched cable TV. In fact less than 10% of the population is connected.

2. Linking words which signal textual relationships

Addition
also, in addition, moreover, furthermore, besides, too, as well as, what's more

Print and visual media are growing, *as well as* computers which can…

Highlight
in particular, in detail, especially, notably, chiefly, mainly

Certain individuals, *notably* Conrad Black, Rupert Murdoch and Sylvio Berlosconi, now dominate the media market.

Stating the obvious
obviously, naturally, of course, clearly

Of course, people will still read a general newspaper and watch a mainstream television channel.

Complete the following text with the appropriate linking words:

Media habits

I get up and turn on the box for the breakfast news. .... I can't hear my newspaper being pushed through the letterbox. As I struggle bleary-eyed downstairs, I can hear the broadcaster solemnly announce an increase in the number of unemployed. .... I determine to remain optimistic in my search for a job. .... there are very few grounds for optimism .... I've been looking for a job for more than a year now. As I munch my way through a bowl of cornflakes, I start to skim through the job advertisements – .... there's practically nothing that would suit me. .... I note down the telephone number of a job hotline which I've not seen before. When I phone them later that morning, I get through to an answerphone telling me to fax them my curriculum vitae .... a letter indicating my job prefer-ences .... salary range. The message ends by requesting a registration fee of $50. Not surprisingly I decide against pursuing this line of enquiry with an answering service.

Putting it all together

Take two or three English language publications (newspapers, magazines) and review them in these terms:

- balance of human stories versus hard news
- comparison of same story in different publications

WORD CHECK 4

to gather come together

glibly smoothly, easily, not sincerely

to be at hand be about to happen

mainstream not specialist or individualized

to come across meet, discover

tier level

to hunt search

to converge come together

to embark start

claim statement

to undermine weaken, make less powerful

mogul very powerful person

Postscript

'I think it's wonderful. I don't have to leave the house. I work from home using fax, modem and computer, I get all my entertainment here and even do my shopping through the computer link-up.'

10 The Environment

The environment continues to be one of the world's major human concerns. But how real are these concerns? From the comfort of our living room, we can see how scientists have brought order to our world and security to our lives. If we compare our existence to that of our ancestors, we have never been safer – from famine, from disease, and from a whole range of natural disasters. Yet there are still those who tell us loudly and passionately that manipulation of the environment may bring short-term benefits, but also spells long-term disaster for the whole planet. So, are we about to return to the Dark Ages?

In this dossier we'll look at whether we represent a threat to the environment or vice versa, and whether the environmentalists are scaremongers or life-preservers.

Features

1 Here is the news:
Hurricane! A radio report

2 Being aware:
How green are you?

3 The right of reply:
Sermons or survival?

4 A healthy balance?
To add or not to add

Getting started

'If science has taught us anything at all, it is that the environment is full of uncertainties.'
Charles Windsor, Prince of Wales

'Unless man can make new and original adaptations to his environment as rapidly as science can change the environment, our culture will perish.'
Carl R Rogers (1902-1987), US psychologist

'Change the environment; do not try to change man.'
Richard Buckminster Fuller (1895-1983), US engineer, educator, philosopher and writer

The above comments indicate the delicate balance between humans and nature. How would you define this relationship? Who is the master and who is the servant?

Hurricane! A radio report

The reporter:

Name of hurricane:

First area affected:

Height of wave:

Estimated casualties:

Type of disaster:

The environmentalist:

Three types of extreme weather events:

Three examples of environmental damage:

Four issues for Earth Summit:

Listen to the news report about the effects of a violent storm. As you listen complete the notes in the table above.

Getting it right

Look at the following sentences from the news broadcast:

> Satellite pictures **enabled** us to watch events as they were unfolding.
> You **can** probably still hear its devastating force outside the hotel.
> The strong winds at present **are preventing** many people from going out.
> Our planet will **be incapable of** sustaining us and it will die.

The table below shows the range of expressions which can convey possibility and ability, and their opposites.

Expressing possibility …	Expressing impossibility …
make able/possible	make unable/impossible
enable	prohibit
allow	prevent
permit	stop
… or ability	**… or inability**
can	can't
be able to	be not able/unable to
capable of	be incapable of

Rewrite the following sentences, replacing the words in italics with one of the expressions in the table. Make any other changes necessary.

1. The summit will *(make it possible)* for world leaders to discuss environmental issues.
2. The terms of the conference *(make it impossible)* for the leaders to take decisions on global environmental actions.
3. As we have seen, the leaders have been *(unable to)* reach a consensus.
4. On another occasion, the industrial lobby would have been *(able to)* influence the decisions.
5. The level of concern will *(make it impossible)* for them to avoid the issues.
6. Yesterday, the police *(made it impossible)* for protesters to enter the conference area. (Start with: Yesterday, protesters were …)

Now write six sentences of your own about the possibility of improving the environment, and your ability to contribute to any improvements.

Word power

The most common verbs of speaking are:

say tell talk speak discuss

Use them in the following sentences, as appropriate:

1. We will .... these questions at the forthcoming conference.
2. To .... the truth, I am quite encouraged by the present situation.
3. The scientists .... that they planned to reduce emissions by 10%.
4. Professor MacDonald will .... at the beginning of the conference about the dangers of global warming.
5. The participants .... late into the night about possible solutions.

Other verbs of speaking are used in specific contexts. Choose the most appropriate verb from the box to complete the sentences below:

accept	declare	prove
add	disclose	reply
allege	emphasize	report
argue	indicate	suggest
comment	notify	transmit

1. I .... that we discuss the points in the following order.
2. I'm afraid I cannot .... that information because it is confidential.
3. I hereby .... the meeting closed.
4. After many hours of discussion they finally .... our proposals.
5. Let me .... once again how important I consider this matter to be.
6. I would like to .... another point to the agenda, namely the benefits brought by modern science.
7. I feel that I must .... to the criticisms made by the previous speakers.
8. The protesters .... that industry has destroyed the environment.

Discussion

In the news item on Hurricane Herbert, Paul Greenslade from Eco2000 finished by saying:

> *The Earth Summit must urgently address the issues of protecting the earth's air, soil, water, and living organisms.*

Discuss what should be done in one or more of these areas. During the discussion, make notes of the main points raised.

Environment at risk?

WORD CHECK 1

famine severe food shortage

scaremonger person who spreads frightening reports of approaching disaster

utter complete

to unfold open to view

wake here, path or territory passed over by flood or other natural disaster

toll here, cost in losses (people or property) after a natural disaster

round the clock twenty-four hours a day

to loot steal, especially from a city conquered by war or other disaster

arch critic main critic

wilful intentional *(AmE: willful)*

drought severe water shortage

to spell something out say or show something clearly

to deforest cut down the trees

to overgraze allow animals to graze (eat grass) to the point of destroying the grazing land

throes *(pl.)* struggle, especially before the onset of death

pole one of the two extremities of the earth's axis, i.e., the north pole and the south pole

reappraisal new valuation, assessment

Getting started

Which environmental issues do you think these icons represent?
Do any of them affect you?

How green are you?

This questionnaire looks at the 'greenness' of your habits.

		YES	NO
1.	Do you generally shower rather than take a bath in order not to waste water?	☐	☐
2.	Do you belong to a car-share scheme so that you can reduce the consumption of fuel?	☐	☐
3.	Do you use a bicycle, whenever possible, instead of a car to conserve energy reserves?	☐	☐
4.	Do you help to save the rain forests by not using tropical hardwood in your home?	☐	☐
5.	Do you turn down your heating, and, if cold, put on more clothes?	☐	☐
6.	Do you recycle paper, glass and aluminium?	☐	☐
7.	Do you use unleaded petrol?	☐	☐
8.	Do you own (or would you buy) a fridge with reduced CFCs (chlorofluorocarbons)?	☐	☐
9.	Do you reduce your speed when driving to lower your energy consumption?	☐	☐
10.	Do you use public transport whenever possible?	☐	☐
11.	Do you buy recycled paper products whenever possible?	☐	☐
12.	Do you select cruelty-free cosmetics and toiletries?	☐	☐

Evaluation: The more YES answers, the greener you are.
If you have more than 3 NO answers, you are a risk to the planet.

Discussion

- Compare your answers and discuss in what ways you think you need to become more environmentally-conscious.
- How seriously do you think such surveys should be treated?

Word power

'Fridge' is a short form of the word 'refrigerator'.

The following words are better known by their short forms. What are these?

advertisement	influenza
examination	high fidelity
photograph	telephone
aeroplane *(BrE)*	bicycle
gasoline *(AmE)*	television
omnibus	motion picture *(AmE)*
condominium *(AmE)*	personal computer

WORD CHECK   2

green   environmentally-conscious, active in solving environmental problems

car-share   system where a group of people travel in the same car rather than in individual cars, especially when going to work *(AmE: car pool)*

reserves   quantity of something kept for future use, eg minerals left in the ground

to recycle   treat a substance in a way so that it can be reused

aluminium   *(AmE: aluminum)* light, soft metal widely used as a container for drinks

textiles   woven cloth or fabric

fridge   refrigerator, large container for keeping food or drinks at very low temperatures

cruelty-free   not tested in a way which causes pain to animals

cosmetics   *(pl.)* preparations applied to a person's skin to preserve the skin or improve its appearance

toiletries   *(pl.)* articles or preparations used in personal hygiene – soap, deodorant, toothpaste, etc.

Getting started

'Animals are locked into their environment; only man with his imagination, his reason, his emotional subtlety and toughness has the ability to change the environment. And that series of inventions by which man from age to age has remade his environment is a kind of evolution – not biological, but cultural.'

Jacob Bronowski, (1908-74),
British scientist and writer

In what ways has man's imagination, reason, emotional subtlety and toughness improved the environment? What inventions have had the greatest impact on the environment in which you live?

Read the following open letter written by Alfred Litho, the leader of Eco-spiracy, a world movement which promotes the free and unlimited use of the environment.

Sermons or survival?

DEAR ENVIRONMENTALISTS,
The recent Rome summit on the environment has provided you and your motley crowd of supporters with yet another opportunity to preach your sermon on the end of the world. However, I wonder why you have pointed the finger firmly at the traditional enemy of politicians and industrialists, without mentioning the many success stories of the last 2000 years. Could you please let me set the record straight?

The natural resources of water, air, food and energy are scientifically classified as either renewable or non-renewable.

Living resources – animals and plants – can reproduce or renew themselves; minerals and fuels cannot. Most natural resources are renewable. If water is polluted, it must be replaced by unpolluted water and measures must be intro-

duced to prevent a recurrence of the problem. This is exactly what our water treatment plants do.

Air pollution, too, must be (and is being) controlled in the same way by the co-operative efforts of government, business and private citizens.

The third resource, food, is available in super-abundant quantities. There is no shortage in terms of production – only difficulties in terms of distribution.

The final resource, energy, needs special treatment, because it is non-renewable and care is needed to conserve it for our descendants.

However, more important even than the basic facts about life on earth is that you have failed to recognize that man's very adaptability has meant his survival. Our ancestors faced the danger of death by disease, attack by wild

animals and the vagaries of their natural environment.

Today's descendants inhabit a world in which many of these risks have been reduced or eliminated. The world is constantly changing and the reason why homo sapiens survives as a species is because of his ability both to change the environment as well as to adapt to the changes.

Earlier life systems also adapted to the shattering changes at the end of the most recent ice age. And there is no reason why our ecosystem will not do the same.

Finally, I get the feeling that you actually relish your negative message. I say that you should accept the challenge and work towards changing the planet, rather than administering its last rites.

Yours sincerely,
Alfred Litho

When you have read the letter, answer these questions:

1. Who are the environmentalists' traditional enemies?
2. Which are the renewable natural resources?
3. In what way does man differ from all other species?

A question of style

In his letter, Alfred Litho used the following forms:

> *I wonder why you have pointed the finger firmly at the traditional enemy of politicians and industrialists.*
> (indirect question)

> *Could you please let me set the record straight?*
> (indirect request)

The first form above typically includes a question word and is a **request for information** (who, what, when, why, where or how). The second form is a **request for action**.

 On your recording you will hear four requests. Indicate in the box opposite whether they are requests for information (I) or action (A)

1.
2.
3.
4.

Now look at how the phrases below change the request for action (A) and information (I) from **direct** to **indirect**:

Direct	Neutral	Indirect
Please + order (A)...		
Please tell me (I)...		
I want you to (A)...	Do you think you could (A)...?	I wonder if you could (A)...?
Do you know (I)...?		
Can you (A)...?	Do you think you could tell me (I)...?	I wonder if you could tell me (I)...?
Can you tell me (I)...?		
I'd like you to (A)...		
I'd like to know (I)...		

You are going to hear eight requests related to environmental topics. In each case the request is either direct, neutral or indirect. Write the number of the exchange under the appropriate heading in the box below.

The first one has been done for you.

Direct	Neutral	Indirect
	1	

Word power

The suffixes **-able** and **-ible** are used to convert verbs to adjectives. For example:

renew – renewable   *exhaust – exhaustible*

What words ending in **-able** or **-ible** have the following meanings?

Something which:

can be repaired	gives enjoyment
can be done	is worth a lot of money
is fit to eat	is preferred
changes often	can be divided
can be broken	

Look at your list of adjectives. For which ones can you form a negative by adding a prefix?

Discussion

Discuss and debate two or more of the following propositions:

1. We worry too much about the environment.
2. We are the master; the environment is the servant.
3. We should all enjoy the environment.

WORD CHECK   3

subtlety art of being very clever in noticing and understanding

motley mixed with both good and bad elements

recurrence repetition

super-abundant more than enough

vagary uncertainty

shattering shocking

to relish get enjoyment, usually from something negative

to administer the last rites *(pl.)* to perform a religious ceremony for a person's death

Getting started

> # PRAWN COCKTAIL FLAVOUR CORN SNACK
>
> **Ingredients: Maize Meal • Vegetable Oil • Starch • Prawn Cocktail Flavour (Acidity Regulator E262, Flavour Enhancer 621, Citric Acid, Flavouring, Artificial Sweetener, Saccharin) • Sugar • Salt • Colours (E110, E160b)**

Do you think that the use of chemicals in food products in your country is increasing, decreasing or remaining stable?

To add or not to add?

In this interview, Jean-Luc Dubois, a nutritionist working for a multinational food company, explains the uses of chemical additives in some of the foods we eat.

Listen to the interview and answer the following questions.

Part 1
1. How does Jean-Luc prefer to describe the chemicals used in food production? How does he justify this description?
2. List three of the chemical agents he mentions.
3. What is the main purpose of these agents, according to Jean-Luc?

Part 2
4. What reasons does Jean-Luc provide to show that chemical agents are not harmful to humans? Try to list three reasons.
5. How does he explain the people who campaign against food chemicals? What particular motive does he attribute to them?

Part 3
6. Listen to Jean-Luc's thoughts about the future use of chemicals in food. Then try to express them in your own words.

Discussion

In the interview you heard about the benefits of using additives in food products. What do you think about their use? Do you agree that they don't do us any harm?

Putting it all together

In this dossier we've explored some emotive issues connected with the environment. You can collect some further information now, by doing a project regarding attitudes about the environment. You should try to get as wide a range of opinions as possible on the subject. Here's how you should proceed.

1. Design a questionnaire to collect attitudes toward environmental issues.
2. Collect the data from about ten people of different ages and from different social backgrounds.
3. Prepare a written report collating the results of your survey.
4. Present and discuss the results of your survey in class.

WORD CHECK   4

emulsifier   something which changes one liquid into another

anti-cracking agent   something to stop the product from breaking

shelf-life   length of storage capacity

allergy   irritation caused by extreme sensitivity to something

food chain   series of organisms dependent on one another for food

outspoken   here, strong in their complaints

vociferous   loud

distorted   misrepresented, or changed in form

synthetic   artificial

enzyme   substance which can cause chemical change in the body

---

Postscript

A visiting student's impression of life in the UK:

'The environmental movement is very strong in Britain. Their chief preoccupations seem to be their gardens, their pets and their families – in that order.'

11 The Law

Our perceptions of the law invariably extend beyond the general idea of regulating conduct in an organized society. Just as legal systems vary from country to country, so do the rights and obligations of individuals within those systems.

How do we regard those who implement these rules – or those who have dedicated their lives to breaking them?

In this dossier we'll explore some of the serious and humorous aspects of lawmakers and lawbreakers.

Features

1 Origins of law:
Organizing Adamsville

2 Practices of law:
How fair is the jury system?

3 Legal systems:
Constitutions and procedures

4 Criminal masterclass:
White collar crime

Getting started

How would you use the following terms to describe your view of the law?

protection   control   empowerment   order   justice   rights

Organizing Adamsville

This light-hearted allegory from *The Lawful Rights of Mankind* by Paul Sieghart reconstructs the possible origins of lawmaking.

We take up the story in Adamsville, where Adam and Eve, Cain and Abel, and their neighbours are living a (fairly) idyllic existence. The village community has already discovered that there are some things they can do much better together than separately, for example, hunting. They also will have found out that some members of the community are better at hunting, others at gathering roots or nuts, and still others at fashioning tools and weapons. The community is beginning to develop a structure, with different members performing different functions. But these functions will need to be coordinated. The hunters will, therefore, get together to plan their tactics, the gatherers to exchange news of what is growing where, the tillers to decide where they will plant which crops. Decisions will need to be made and advice given in difficult circumstances. But so far there are no rulers and no ruled, no leaders or led, no landlords or serfs.

Then one day a major catastrophe befalls the community – a shortage of food. For the first time, some members of the community are forced to go hungry.

Until this shortage, there was no need for anyone to make any claims against anyone else. But in this time of shortage, it is no longer so. Everyone is making conflicting claims against everyone else. Nimrod claims he is entitled to more food because his band has killed more wild animals than the others; Absalom maintains that, having broken his ankle while gathering fruit in a tree, the others should feed him while his disability lasts.

How will they deal with problems like these? In essence they have two options: competition or cooperation. If they compete, then the strongest will take what they need and survive; the rest will go short, fall sick and eventually die.

On the other hand, if they all cooperate, they will share what there is according to some sensible scheme, and then there is a reasonable prospect that all, or most, of them will survive.

Let us suppose that Adamsville chooses cooperation and survives. But they realize that they need to be better prepared for a crisis next time around. They need sensible plans to handle shortage and trouble. A meeting is called.

The agenda consists of the following points:

1. Who is to decide what the rules should say?
2. Who is going to apply them to the various individual claims?
3. How can one ensure that no one will break them?

Role Play

Imagine you are at the meeting in Adamsville. Discuss the points on the above agenda.

Word power

The word **tactics** is one of a group of nouns ending in **-ics** (with a plural 's'). It is followed by a plural verb:

These tactics are always successful.

However, sometimes nouns ending in **-ics** are treated as singular nouns and are followed by a singular verb:

Statistics is a subject of study based on systematically organizing numerical data.

Usually, where the noun is the name of an academic subject or an abstract concept, we use a singular verb; otherwise, we use a plural verb.

The statistics show a remarkable rise in crime.

Which words ending in **-ics** have the following meanings?

science and art of government
study of the production and distribution of wealth
abstract science of space, number and quantity
set of morals and moral principles
science of sound
practice of and competition in physical exercises
science of language

Idyllic (from the noun **idyll**) is one of a group of adjectives ending in **-ic**.

Physical (from the noun **physique**) is one of a group of adjectives ending in **-ical**.

Find the correct adjectives for the nouns below:

drama	critic
theory	magic
hero	science
practice	grammar
system	sympathy

Both **-ic** and **-ical** adjectives form adverbs with **-ally**:
idyll, idyllic, idyllically,
physique, physical, physically
The one exception is *public,* where *publicly* is preferred to
publically.

WORD CHECK   1

perception view, understanding
conduct behaviour
obligation duty
to implement put into practice
idyllic pleasant because of its natural
    beauty
to fashion make, form
tiller person who grows crops by turning
    the soil and sowing seeds

serf slave
to befall happen (usually of sad or
    negative events)
to be entitled to have the right to
to maintain claim strongly
disability inability to work because
    of physical or mental handicap

Getting started

Some people believe that the law protects the rights of the individual, others believe it protects the elite and contributes to the polarization of society.

What attitudes to the law are shown in the quotations below? Do they present an accurate picture of the law?

'There's one law for the rich, and one law for the poor.'

English proverb

'The majestic egalitarianism of the law, which forbids rich and poor alike to sleep under bridges, to beg in the streets and to steal bread …'

Anatole France (1844-1924), French novelist and critic

How fair is the jury system?

1. The worst jury

A murder trial at Manitoba in 1978 was well-advanced, when one juror revealed that he was completely deaf and did not have the remotest clue what was happening.

The judge, Mr Justice Solomon, asked him if he had heard any evidence at all and, when there was no reply, dismissed him.

The excitement which this caused was only equalled when a second juror revealed that he spoke not a word of English. A fluent French speaker, he exhibited great surprise when told, after two days, that he was hearing a murder trial.

The trial was finally abandoned when a third juror said that he suffered from both conditions. The judge ordered a retrial.

2. A country jury

A man was on trial in a small town in New South Wales for stealing some heifers. The jury was made up of the defendant's neighbours.

When they returned from their deliberations with their verdict, they were asked: 'Do you find this man guilty or not guilty of cattle stealing?' The foreman replied: 'Not guilty, if he returns the cows.'

The jury was sent away to 'find a true verdict according to the evidence.' When they returned, they had a belligerent air about them. 'Have you decided on your verdict?' 'Yes', replied the foreman. 'We find the accused not guilty and he doesn't have to return the cows.'

The Book of Heroic Failures
by Stephen Pile

3. The jury system in action

In England, serious criminal trials are heard by a judge and jury. The English judicial system operates on the basis of a separation of powers. The judge is there to decide on questions of law (what exactly the statute or offence means and requires); while the jury has to decide on questions of fact – whether the defendant has really broken the terms of the law which the judge has outlined to them.

The idea is that twelve men and women, who have no prior knowledge of the case, the defendant or the witnesses, listen to the evidence and give a dispassionate verdict. It is a concept of which we are justly proud, and one which we use as a yardstick of judicial fairness to measure against other countries' systems.

However, in 1967, the centuries-old safeguard of a unanimous verdict in jury trials was abolished. Thereafter a defendant could be convicted on a 10–2 majority verdict. This makes a legal mockery of the theory of English criminal justice that the case must be proved beyond all reasonable doubt. Now the reasonable doubt of two can be conveniently discounted.

What's Wrong with Your Rights?
by Roger Cook and Tim Tate

1. In the first extract, how could the situation in the trial have been avoided?
2. In the second extract on the previous page, why do you think the jurors returned their first verdict?
3. In the final extract, on what grounds do the authors claim that English criminal justice has been compromised?

Discussion

You might conclude from the extracts that the jury system fails to serve its purpose of convicting the guilty and acquitting the innocent. What system applies in your country? Do you think there is a fairer way to decide the questions of guilt and innocence?

Getting it right

A **complex sentence** consists of more than one clause and more than one verb phrase. The clauses can be linked either by coordination or subordination.

Coordination is quite straightforward, using conjunctions such as **and, or, but:**

> *We find the accused not guilty and he doesn't have to return the cows.* (linked by coordinating conjunction 'and')

Subordination may be more complicated. It involves two or more clauses joined by a subordinating conjunction. Some typical examples are shown here:

> *that   if   as   when   (al)though   because*

> **When** *they returned, they had a belligerent air about them.* (subordinate clause followed by main clause)

> *The idea is* **that** *twelve men and women listen to the evidence.* (main clause followed by subordinate clause)

Combine the following sentences or clauses using subordination and making any other necessary changes. Your sentence should have the same meaning as the original.

1. A jury is a group of laymen. They decide factual issues in criminal and civil trials. *(subordination with a 'wh' word)*
2. The jury was used in non-Anglo-American countries. However, it lost power and became far less common in the 19th and early 20th centuries.
3. Jury trials occur most frequently in the United States. Ninety per cent of all jury trials in the world are held there. *(subordination with a 'wh' word)*

4. Some individuals may be biased. Therefore they are excluded from jury service.
5. In Europe, a two-thirds majority must agree that a defendant is guilty; if not, he must be acquitted.
6. In criminal cases, the jury's duty is to decide questions of fact; on the other hand, in civil trials they decide matters of liability and levels of damages.

Word power

The three reading extracts in this section deal with legal procedures and people involved with the law.

Read through the extracts again and find suitable words to list under these headings:

Legal procedures   **People involved with the law**

Now complete the following sentences using the words from your list.

1. A person is put on .... for an offence that he or she is alleged to have committed.
2. The person who stands trial for a criminal offence is called the ....
3. In a criminal trial .... may be called to give ....
4. In a civil .... the person against whom the complaint is made is called the ....
5. A .... is usually composed of 12 men and women from the community and one of them acts as the ....
6. Some professionals, such as policemen and lawyers, are exempt from serving as ....
7. After the evidence has been heard, the jury retires to decide upon the ....
8. Finally, in criminal trials, the .... passes sentence.

Getting it right

Punctuation includes the proper use of: capital letters, commas (,), full stops/periods (.), colons (:), semi-colons (;), quotation marks (""), exclamation marks (!), question marks (?) and apostrophes (').

The **comma** has few hard and fast rules, but it is used generally to make reading easier:

However, in 1967, the centuries-old safeguard of a unanimous verdict in jury trials was abolished.

Note that a comma is not used in English before a subordinate clause starting with 'that':

One juror revealed that he was completely deaf.

The **colon** is a simpler matter: it goes between independent clauses, where the second explains or fulfils the first, or before a list:

In essence they have two options: competition or cooperation.

The **semi-colon** usually replaces or precedes an adverbial link such as 'however', 'in addition', 'while':

The judge is there to decide on questions of law; the jury has to decide on questions of fact.

Now punctuate the following single sentence by Samuel Leibowitz, an American lawyer, on selecting a jury. You might want to read the sentence out loud before punctuating it.

---

avoid writers because they
invariably construct their own case based upon
dramatic values and ignore the law and the facts professors and those
who live cloistered lives generally because they are too easily
shocked by the raw facts of life former policemen and private
watchmen because the chances are that at one time
or another they have been
outwitted by criminals

WORD CHECK   2

polarization   separation into two diametrically opposed positions

egalitarianism   belief that all men are equal and should have equal access to rights and privileges in society

to plead (guilty/not guilty)   claim to be

statute   a law enacted by government

dispassionate   calm in judgement, uninfluenced by prejudice

yardstick   measure

safeguard   protection

to convict   find guilty

mockery   insincere imitation

to discount   ignore

deliberation   careful consideration

foreman   leader of a group, here, of the jury

belligerent   hostile, unfriendly

clue   idea

Getting started

Divorce is part of family law. What branches of law do the following words come from?

palimony

breach of contract

trespass

theft

FAMILY LAW
COMMERCIAL LAW
CRIMINAL LAW
CIVIL LAW

bigamy

unfair dismissal

negligence

murder

Constitutions and procedures

Listen to the five speakers talking about various systems of law. As you listen, complete the notes in the table below.

Extract	Subject discussed	Main points
1	.... constitution	Three advantages:
2	.... constitution	Main advantage:
3	.... law	Purpose:
4	....	Under inquisitorial system: Under adversarial system:
5	.... vs	Results: Speaker's view:

A question of style

Study the techniques that the speakers used to emphasize the following words and phrases:

Two major points I would consider important: first, …
(emphasis at beginning of the sentence)

Not only does he do this during the trial, but also before.
(inversion)

In fact, it is the judge who decides whether to prosecute or not.
(relative clause)

What differentiates the two systems is more a question of origins and procedures rather than substance.
(relative clause)

Rewrite the following sentences to emphasize the words in italics.

1. Both parties can *interrogate the witnesses.*
2. *The citizen* benefits from not having a written constitution.
3. We can see differences *in the legal procedures.*
4. Each side tries to *prove their case.*
5. The adversarial system ensures a fairer trial, *and* provides a quicker one.
6. The law should give *justice for all.*

Now write six sentences about the law and its role in society. You should use different forms to emphasize your points.

Discussion

Imagine that you have been asked to draft guidelines for legal proceedings in Adamsville. (See pp. 120-121.)

First discuss what should be the true purpose of legal proceedings.

- Should it be to find out the facts of what really happened, as in the continental legal system you heard about?
- Or should it be simply to find out whether an accused person has done what is alleged, as in the English legal system?

In other words, should legal proceedings aim to establish what really happened or just prove beyond reasonable doubt what is claimed to have happened?

 Now draft a set of recommendations for the Adamsville elders to follow.

WORD CHECK   3

doctrine　an agreed principle
to confer　give
I am bound to say　legalistic phrase meaning 'I believe strongly that …'
minutiae　small details
to be derived from　originate from
to elevate　raise
piecemeal　one piece at a time, gradually

advocate　lawyer who presents the case of another in court
to interrogate　ask detailed questions
a string of　a lot of
barrister　in the English legal system, a lawyer who represents the client in a higher court of law
to acquit　find not guilty

Getting started

POLICE GAVE CHASE to the robbers as they left the bank and headed for the border.

A MASSIVE FRAUD has recently been uncovered by detectives investigating the computer systems department at National Bank headquarters.

What two faces of crime do these two news items illustrate? Which do you regard as the more serious or more dangerous crime?

White collar crime

Mike Feilding is a computer consultant and advises companies and organizations on secure computer installations. In this recorded interview, he discusses the spread of computer-assisted crime: who commits it, and what the public perception of it is.

Listen to the interview and complete the notes below:

Part 1

1. Reasons for spread of computer crime   *All sorts of people …*
2. Example of computer frauds
3. Insiders or outsiders to blame?

Part 2

4. How easy to detect or prevent?
5. What sort of punishments?

Part 3

6. Measures suggested to protect security
7. Why public doesn't take this crime more seriously
8. What chance of eradicating white collar crime?

In the interview, Mike told a story about a paying-in slip fraud. Listen again to this section of the recording, and then re-write the story in your own words, as if for a magazine or newspaper.

You could begin with the headline:

JUDGE FINES COMPUTER TRICKSTER JUST $1!

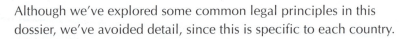
Discussion

Mike Feilding confirmed that white-collar crime, and particularly computer-assisted crime, is growing rapidly. But, as he said, people still don't take it very seriously. Do you agree? Should we be more concerned about what is being done 'far away with numbers we don't understand and technology we don't understand either'? What sort of penalties would you impose for convicted white-collar criminals?

Putting it all together

Although we've explored some common legal principles in this dossier, we've avoided detail, since this is specific to each country.

One way of finding out more about your own legal system is to interview a number of professionals to find out their precise duties. You could then add the information to this dossier to reflect the current legal practices in your country.

Finally, present and discuss this information in class.

WORD CHECK 4

chitties *(BrE)* small pieces of paper

weeping and wailing *(colloq.)* crying and complaining, very unhappy

furore uproar, loud complaining

to hack in process of illegally gaining entry into another's computer system

mayhem chaos

slip small piece of paper, see *chitty*

to monitor keep track of

rogue here, illegal, unauthorized

to mete out (punishment) to hand out

to shuffle here, to move around dishonestly

stiff (penalty) heavy

malevolent intent intention to do wrong

not moved to not feeling the desire to

to log in gain access to a computer file

concept here, way of looking at something

margins outskirts, outside edge

that attaches to personal affront that makes them feel personally offended

to eradicate eliminate

to pick the lock to unlock illegally

Postscript

What is a criminal lawyer?

Someone who specializes in criminal law

A lawyer who is a criminal

12 Entertainment

Whether in the theatre, concert hall, cinema, or through the television at home, entertainment accounts for a significant proportion of our leisure time. It has also attracted huge commercial interests. But how far do these interests influence the type of entertainment that is available? In the sphere of mass entertainment, does 'more' necessarily mean 'better'?

The development of television and home video recording systems has already revolutionized listening and viewing habits; virtual reality promises ever more exciting and elaborate ways of escaping from daily pressures.

But on a human level there are still those individuals who entertain us and strive to create something unique in their work. In this dossier we'll talk to one such entertainer before we turn to the world of books to find out your idea of 'a good read'.

Features

1 What's on TV?
   Pleasing the people?

2 Musical tastes:
   From classics to jazz

3 Future trends:
   The electronic circus

4 A good read:
   Fact or fiction

131

Getting started

- Do you watch much TV?
- If so, what sort of programmes do you prefer?
- If not, why not? What don't you like about TV?

Pleasing the people?

Listen to this extract from a panel discussion about TV. Three people give their views. As you listen, note down their opinions.

Viewer	Opinions
1.	
2.	
3.	

Getting it right

There are various ways of expressing likes and preferences:

Basically, people like to be engaged.
Many viewers would like to be better informed about …
I must admit I don't like missing Casualty.

Like
I like documentaries.
I like watching *Casualty*.
I like to see a range of programmes.
I like the children to stop watching TV at nine.

Would like
I would like to be better informed.
I would like more documentaries.
I would like you to switch off the TV.

Like expresses *general* preferences.
Would like expresses *specific* preferences (at a certain time).

Prefer

I prefer sports programmes to documentaries.

I prefer watching TV to doing housework.

I prefer to record a programme than (to) watch it late.

Rather than watch it late, I prefer to record it.

I prefer such programmes to be shown late.

Would prefer

I would prefer more sports to more documentaries.

I would prefer to watch the other channel.

I would prefer you to watch less TV.

(I would prefer you watched less TV.)

Prefer is used when there are two choices (sometimes only one is mentioned).

Would prefer is used for a hypothetical preference (if you were given the choice).

Complete the sentences by matching the first (1-8) and second (a-h) parts together.

1. Do you like …
2. I would prefer you …
3. I don't like my …
4. Rather than …
5. I quite like …
6. He prefers …
7. His parents prefer the …
8. Would you like …

(a) … watching thrillers, but I really enjoy period drama.
(b) … to watch less television but, if you insist, then I would like you to watch something educational.
(c) … to watch the news. No, I'd prefer something funny.
(d) … listen to the radio, I prefer to watch TV.
(e) … watching the commercials to the actual programmes.
(f) … radio to TV.
(g) … to watch soap operas? I don't mind, but I prefer to watch sports.
(h) … children to watch violent movies.

Word power

Match these programme descriptions with the types of programme listed in the box:

1. In its 20th year, it follows the lives of working class people in an industrial town.
2. A dramatic reconstruction of the rescue at Entebbe airport.
3. Contestants answer questions about words and idioms.
4. Interviews with top celebrities
5. Based on a nineteenth century novel, it tells the story of Meg Richards, a society lady.
6. A comedy programme based around the lives of two medical students.

period drama	quiz show *(AmE: game show)*
chat show *(AmE: talk show)*	soap opera
sitcom	documentary drama

Discussion

• What are your views on the quality of television in your country? (Think about types of programme, commercial/educational, and the impact of advertising.)
• Comment on your favourite programmes or the programmes you never watch.
• What are the viewing habits of your friends and neighbours?

WORD CHECK 1

virtual reality technological re-creation of reality
medium means of communication
to spark ignite, create
ratings measurement of number of viewers watching particular programmes
worthy respectful and serious

arrogant convinced you are right
mindless no intellectual content
escapist allowing escape from reality
light entertainment comedy programmes, soap operas, etc.
missionary having a sense of mission
critical faculties intelligence
sitcom *(abbr.)* situation comedy

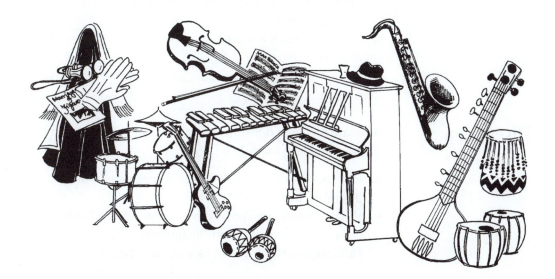

Getting started

- What sort of music do you like?
- Have your musical tastes changed over the years?

From classics to jazz

Meredith White is a New Zealand pianist. Trained in a classical style, she has since turned to playing jazz.

Listen to the interview and fill in the blanks with the expressions Meredith uses.

Part 1

1. Because they weren't .... , she couldn't take up the scholarship.
2. I decided it would be an ....
3. I wasn't all that keen at first … I think it's really ....

Part 2

4. It's a bit like learning a language, in the sense that there's ....
5. … first of all playing a tune, then you ....
6. … for me the main difference between classical music and jazz is that jazz .... in a much stronger way than classical music.

Part 3

7. One of the things I really like about jazz is that it .... and all ages as well.

8. ... the audience is more responsive, because they tend to clap after solos and you ....

9. It's opened a door for me , a .... which I think is very exciting.

Discussion

What are the main differences Meredith points to between playing classical and jazz music?

*   How easy do you feel it would be to change from one discipline to another?
*   What artists do you know of who have 'crossed over' from one branch of the arts to another?
*   How successful do you think they have been?

Sound advice

Look at these three sentences from Meredith's interview:

I'd like to do more writing …
She stayed in New Zealand and taught …
A jazz standard like 'Autumn Leaves' …

We find silent consonants

*   at the beginning of words: *writing, know*
*   in the middle: *taught, foreign*
*   at the end of words: *Autumn, lamb*

How many words can you find with silent consonants?

WORD CHECK 2

an acquired taste something that takes time to learn to enjoy
immersed in totally involved with
genre type or style, particularly in the arts
pulse regular beat

laid down predetermined, fixed
all walks of life from all social classes and occupations
male-dominated controlled by men

Getting started

- How did your grandparents entertain themselves?
- What about the youth of today – how do they spend their leisure time?

The electronic circus

ENTERTAINMENT used to be a communal experience, something available outside the home. Now, at the end of the 20th century, it has taken over the home and transformed its organization. One might predict that in coming decades, a new generation will find a place for entertainment that assists escape from the home and a relief from a world fraught with competitive stress.

There are two parallel trends, of opposite kinds, which may characterize the next era in entertainment. On the one hand, the big spectacular communal experience will return, with stylish venues and media aided by technology; this will become the circus of the 21st century. The prevailing aesthetic will demand the most completely convincing representations, whether of history, contemporary events or fantasy. On the other hand, one will see the virtually inevitable popular acceptance of interactivity. If you attempt to link up these two tendencies, you arrive at a medium of dial-up virtual techniques to gain access to an intangible but wholly enthralling experience, giving the solitary individual the feeling of being present at a spectacle in the illusory company of large numbers of others.

One can also envisage a form of virtual reality available in booths, perhaps in shopping and entertainment areas of cities, and perhaps eventually turning into a home device. It would be the apt culmination of the 20th century's search for profuse and entrancing escapist devices. It could also do much for traditional media such as museums, which could exploit the devices of exact similitude in wonderful ways; one could walk into a gallery displaying artefacts from ancient Greece and be transported back into that time.

Ingenuity in the provision of new forms of entertainment is likely to provide much of the drive for the big technological leaps to come in the 21st century.

The Economist, 11th September, 1993

Read the article above and answer the questions which follow.

1. What will the new generation be seeking?
2. What are the two parallel trends the author predicts?
3. How will these two trends combine?
4. What uses of virtual reality technology does the author predict?

Word power

Look at these combinations of adverbs and adjectives from the article:

Completely convincing representations
Virtually inevitable popular acceptance (of interactivity)

Adverbs	Adjectives
virtually	flawed
fundamentally	close
incredibly	skilled
singularly	impossible
wholly	essential
tantalizingly	predictable
absolutely	unamusing
highly	funny

Combine an adverb and an adjective from these lists to complete the sentences below; several alternatives are possible.

1. The climbers were attempting a .... route up the north face of the mountain.
2. The critics all thought the new series was .... viewing.
3. The match always had a .... outcome.
4. The new system requires .... technicians to maintain it.
5. They supported their request for money on a .... argument.
6. You should see her .... impersonations of leading politicians.
7. Don't bother to turn on the TV. There's a .... comedy programme on at the moment.
8. It was a .... result. They lost in the end by just half a point.

A question of style

'The Electronic Circus' is characterized by a choice of rather formal words. Match some of these words with their more everyday equivalents.

Formal	Informal
1. transform	(a) dominant
2. assist	(b) full of
3. fraught (with)	(c) exciting
4. prevailing	(d) lonely
5. enthralling	(e) delightful
6. solitary	(f) suitable
7. similitude	(g) change
8. apt	(h) help
9. entrancing	(i) likeness

Now try to write appropriate sentences using five formal and five informal words.

Discussion

- Do you think communal entertainment will once again be more popular than home-based entertainment?
- Does the concept of virtual reality excite or frighten you?
- What changes would you like to see in the future world of entertainment?

WORD CHECK   3

communal involving the community, a group of people

fraught (with) accompanied by or full of (especially something negative)

venue place (for an event)

aesthetic taste

interactivity concept of interaction between user and a variety of media

dial-up connected to telephone lines

intangible not concrete, not touchable

illusory imagined, not real

booth small enclosed area for telephoning, voting, etc.

profuse abundant

ingenuity cleverness

Getting started

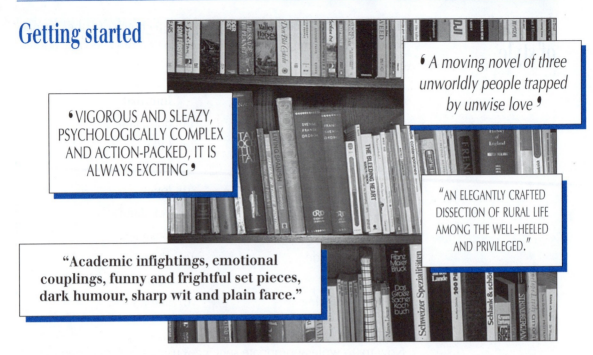

'VIGOROUS AND SLEAZY, PSYCHOLOGICALLY COMPLEX AND ACTION-PACKED, IT IS ALWAYS EXCITING'

'A moving novel of three unworldly people trapped by unwise love'

"AN ELEGANTLY CRAFTED DISSECTION OF RURAL LIFE AMONG THE WELL-HEELED AND PRIVILEGED."

"Academic infightings, emotional couplings, funny and frightful set pieces, dark humour, sharp wit and plain farce."

Here are extracts from the cover blurbs of four different novels.

- Which of them would you most like to read and which least?
- Why?

Fact or fiction

What sort of reader are you? Complete the questionnaire opposite to find out. Then compare your results with a colleague's.

Discussion

- At what time of day do you usually read?
- Describe something you have read recently – was it for work or pleasure?

Cultural connections

Reading habits, like most things, are heavily influenced by parents and education.

In the UK children are brought up to rate certain writers very highly – for example, William Shakespeare (a playwright), Charles Dickens (a novelist), and William Wordsworth (a poet). This does not necessarily mean they enjoy reading the work of these writers.

- Which writers are famous in your country?
- Did your education give you a 'love' of some of these writers?

A READING SURVEY

A. Type of reading matter

1. Which of the following do you read?

☐ – a daily paper
☐ – a weekly/monthly magazine
☐ – novels
☐ – biographies
☐ – non-fiction books

2. In newspapers, which of the following do you enjoy reading most?

☐ – news stories
☐ – editorial and leading articles
☐ – letters to the editor
☐ – obituaries
☐ – business pages
☐ – arts pages
☐ – sports pages
☐ – health/social affairs pages
☐ – gossip columns

3. What type of magazines interest you most?

☐ – general interest
☐ – specialist hobby
☐ – women's magazines
☐ – men's magazines
☐ – others (please specify): ....

4. What type of books do you enjoy most?

☐ – classic fiction
☐ – modern fiction
☐ – non-fiction
☐ – others (please specify): ....

B. Time for reading

5. How much time do you spend reading a week? ....

Interpreting the results:

Part A: Type of reading matter. Count up the marked boxes: 0-5, reluctant reader; 6-10, average reader; 11-15, avid reader; 15+, bookworm.

Part B: Time for reading (hours per week):– 0-1 hour, uninformed; 2-3 hours, informed; 3-4 hours, well-informed; 4+ hours, encyclopaedic.

WORD CHECK 4

blurb short description of a book printed on book jacket or cover

unworldly here, unfamiliar with the world, naive

coupling the sexual act

set piece a staged event

farce a dramatic work designed to make you laugh

well-heeled wealthy

sleazy cheap, squalid and disreputable

obituary notice of a person's death, often including a biographical sketch

gossip often unproven talk about people's private lives

avid eager

bookworm somebody who is always reading a book

Postscript

I've never seen a soap, and in any case only the Italians really understand opera.

Classic literature? What you really mean is boring stories written in language nobody understands.

DOSSIER KEY

Dossier 1	Language & Learning	145
Dossier 2	Food & Drink	153
Dossier 3	The World of Work	164
Dossier 4	Travel	171
Dossier 5	Education	179
Dossier 6	A Question of Sport	189
Dossier 7	International Business	196
Dossier 8	Health	202
Dossier 9	The Media	209
Dossier 10	The Environment	217
Dossier 11	The Law	224
Dossier 12	Entertainment	233

Key 1 — Language & Learning

1   BREAKING THE ICE

Fact or fancy? The birth of language

Comprehension answers:
1. Theory 1.
2. Theories 2, 3 and 6.
3. Theory 5
4. Theory 4.

Word power

Synonyms

spontaneous	primitive
modify	mystically
disgust	consistently
originate	gesture
joy	understandable

Negative prefixes

unpopular	illogical
inhuman	irregularly
impractical	disappear
unmusical	inconsistently
misunderstood	infamous

2   YOU, THE LEARNER

A case for the language doctor?

Answers:
1. Fa'ad   2. Anna   3. Yuki   4. Anders   5. Mariluz

Getting it right

1. I might have studied that last year.
2. Language could have grown out of man's attempts to imitate natural sounds.

3.   People's earliest communication must have been by gesture.

4.   You couldn't have learnt English as a foreign language.

5.   You should have practised more and studied less.

Word power

Noun	Adjective	Verb
belief	believable	believe
weakness	weak	weaken
expression	expressive	express
product/production	productive	produce
advice	advisable	advise
repetition	repetitive	repeat
basis	basic	base
application	applicable	apply
practice*	practical	practise*
recognition	recognizable	recognize
observation	observable	observe

*   In AmE the verb is also spelt with a 'c' – 'practice'

1.   According to the Skinner model, language is learnt by repetition.

2.   The Skinner model cannot explain how children are able to combine words to make expressions they have never heard before.

3.   One rule in language learning is: The more you practise, the more fluent you'll become.

4.   At an advanced level it is advisable to try to extend your vocab-ulary, since words are the main carriers of meaning.

5.   Learners often regard their foreign accent as a weakness, but it is rather a sign of their language origin.

3   WHO'S TALKING?

Voices and views

Extract 1

INTERVIEWER: Matthew, I believe you've just finished your studies. Have you got a job?

MATTHEW: Yes, I've got a job ... not much of one though.

INTERVIEWER: So what are you doing?

MATTHEW: I'm working in a <u>bar serving</u> drinks.

INTERVIEWER: And what did you study?

MATTHEW: I studied physics.

INTERVIEWER: Well I thought that was what we needed … you know, more scientists and all that?

MATTHEW: That's what they told me, too, when I was at school.

INTERVIEWER: So what's the difficulty ... are there just no jobs?

MATTHEW: Well, I'd like to work in research –

INTERVIEWER: Yes?

MATTHEW: – but it seems most companies are cutting back on research at the moment.

INTERVIEWER: So, what's your next step?

MATTHEW: I'm going to try to work abroad … at least that way I'll get some useful experience.

INTERVIEWER: Have you had any offers?

MATTHEW: Yeah, actually I've just heard from a firm in Hamburg – they might take me on as a market researcher.

INTERVIEWER: But that's not really what you had in mind, is it?

MATTHEW: No, but beggars can't be choosers.

Extract 2

REPORTER: This is a very picturesque part of the world and one which the guidebooks all mention. So this must draw a lot of tourists.

ISLANDER: Yes, we've seen major changes in our island since tourists arrived in large numbers. But, we're getting used to seeing them now. It's not a bad thing, as far as I'm concerned.

REPORTER: I'm surprised that you should feel so positive about them.

ISLANDER: Well, I used to object to them. You know, the crowds and the noise. But I've got used to them now. All in all, I think they've been a benefit to the community.

REPORTER: In what way?

ISLANDER: Firstly, cultural. People come from all over to visit us. And they give us a window on the world. It means that we're no longer a backwater, no longer so isolated. Of course, not everybody would agree; some of the locals would prefer them not to come, would like to preserve island life as it was years ago. But, I don't think you can turn back the clocks; I'm all for progress. And then of course, there's the financial side. Visitors spend money here. And that's good for everyone.

Extract 3

Here in France, we and our European Union partners follow what is called the Roman or continental law system, whereas in England the system is called the common law. What differentiates the two systems is more a question of origins and procedures rather than substance. I mean, under both systems, there is the rule of law. However, the Roman system is derived from the formal written codes – such as the ones the Romans had. The Romans, you see, during the expansion of their empire, tried to keep all of their territories under a unified system of law. Of course, they were administered locally by the magistrates. But the state was considered a powerful force – elevated above individuals and their rights.

Extract 4

REPORTER: Apartheid in sport was the most visible symbol of the prejudices which dominated South Africa. How have things changed recently?

COACH: They've changed a lot. But you've got to understand it's not just a question of throwing out the old apartheid laws which prevented blacks from playing with whites. Success in sport is all about opportunity. The opportunity to start playing when you're young, the time to practise, the facilities to be available. There's a lot still to be done, but you can see some changes. Blacks are playing more cricket, there are one or two black players in the regional rugby teams –

REPORTER: Well, surely one or two black rugby players is not much to be proud about? What about providing those opportunities you talked about?

COACH: Well, that's a long-term process. It's not just a question of changing attitudes, it's also improving the standard of living of most black people. You're hardly going to become a top-class sportsman if you're unemployed and living in a shanty town.

Extract 5

I don't mind them hounding politicians and the like to an early grave or more likely resignation – they chose public life and so they have to live in the public eye. No, what I can't stand is the way the tabloids pick on the private individual. Just the other day, there was a story about a young mother who had had to give up her two children – it was splashed all over the paper, taking a moralising tone as usual.

Extract 1   The World of Work
Extract 2   Travel
Extract 3   The Law
Extract 4   A Question of Sport
Extract 5   The Media

**A question
of style**

The origins of the speakers:
1. UK
2. An island in the Caribbean
3. France
4. South Africa
5. India

4   HOW TO SAY IT

Applying the magic

Part 1

INTERVIEWER: Nigel, what do you think the – the relationship is, if
there is any, between natural talent and training and practice when
it comes to – to acting, performing in public?

NIGEL LAMBERT: Well I think that all actors have a natural talent to
start with, but you need to have training for the technique side of it
because for example – you may be a wonderful King Lear, but you
couldn't play King Lear for perhaps more than two nights, if you
haven't had some vocal training, because your voice just won't
take it, and by the third night it's gone. So you've got to learn to
reserve and to learn to harness and channel – that's the technique
side, so that's what I would say.

INTERVIEWER: And is that very different, do you think, from talking
normally?

NIGEL LAMBERT: Oh very different. I think when you first begin to do
it – holding, pulling out your rib cage and then just pushing in with
your diaphragm to let the air come out is very strange the first time,
but it means you can do long sentences without having to take a
breath and you can keep going and going and going.

INTERVIEWER: Right, yes, so that's in terms of verbal communication
and acting; what about in terms of body language, body acting –
how important is that?

NIGEL LAMBERT: It's very important, but I do think that body language

– if the thinking is right as an actor or as a performer in a communication that you're giving across – if that's right, then the body language will go with it. If you have a thought in your mind, a strong thought but you're sitting back with your legs crossed – you think 'Just a minute, why is his body like that but he's saying that?'– something is wrong and I think that's 'acting'. It's – it's a little bit phoney because really, you should be perhaps sitting forward, your voice is raised, your gestures are large because you have a large and important thing to say.

Part 2

INTERVIEWER: Coming back to verbal language, how important do you think the words are themselves in conveying meaning?

NIGEL LAMBERT: Oh of paramount importance. I mean the words are the most important thing of all, and as an actor it's harder – it's harder work for us to make a poor play work than a good play. If a play is well-written it carries itself and you just kind of push it this way, push it that way. It's the poor plays you've got to really work hard at. So yes, words are the most important thing of all.

INTERVIEWER: And what about the delivery of those words? I mean, again, are there techniques that you can learn to, er …?

NIGEL LAMBERT: Well it's all to do with variety it seems to me … where I think, people in business, – I train people in business as well as being an actor – and where they don't have the actor's natural inclination is to be aware of variety and the need for variety, it just drones on a bit page after page after page and the audience just switch off.

INTERVIEWER: These are businessmen giving presentations at conferences or whatever?

NIGEL LAMBERT: Yes, and conventions, that's right. And what they don't seem to have that actors have inbuilt, is a sense of variety. They keep the ball in the air all the time, they change the pace, they change the volume, they change the attack, everything – everything is just kept alive, but business people – over the years I've found – tend to just drone on page after page after page which is very sad. It's a bit like taking a motorway journey, say a hundred mile journey. You could go on the motorway which is very quick, you'll be there in half the time, but you could take the little side roads, the little – the roundabouts, the villages, the little ponds; you slow down here, you speed up there, it might take you longer, but as an audience sitting in the back seat of that car, it's a much more enjoyable journey. And also I find that most business people, because they're very busy people, they don't write their own speeches, they have a writer write them for them – their number two writes it for them – and the sadness is that the words aren't really their own words, and it sounds a bit stilted and staid, it's not their own flow.

INTERVIEWER: So what's the trick of it then, I mean how can somebody deliver something which is not natural to them?

NIGEL LAMBERT: Well to be them – they have to be themselves, that's the most important thing of all. It's the old thing I know, but they have to be themselves. The audience have to see the person they believe – they expect to see. But the message has to be shaped and phrased in a way that will excite them. It has to … have variety, it has to have build. It starts here, moves to there, moves to there, and finally goes to there. But it has to be Charlie Smith on that stage and they must believe it's Charlie Smith, not someone imposing something on himself.

INTERVIEWER: So although they can use some techniques of an actor in terms of variety and intonation, they – you're not suggesting it's a good idea for them to use the full acting techniques of projection and seeking a different personality?

NIGEL LAMBERT: Absolutely not, absolutely not, it isn't to do with acting, it isn't acting. What, I think, the audience in a business wants to see, what the delegates want to see, is the boss man up there giving a sincere message, and if he is fired up by something he must look to be fired up and only that way will they be fired up.

Part 3

INTERVIEWER: So Nigel we've talked a lot about presenting language in formal context, whether it's acting on the stage or presenting in conferences and so on. What about on a more informal level and just actually speaking a language, what sort of tricks of the trade or tools of the trade do you think you could pass on to people who are learning a language?

NIGEL LAMBERT: Well, you know we talked about variety earlier, and variety is so important and certainly in the speaking of a foreign language, speaking English, variety is everything. It's no good just knowing the words and the phrases, that's great but it's awfully boring. So to get real colour and fun from a language you've got to study as well the intonations and er …

INTERVIEWER: In order to get across what you want to say.

NIGEL LAMBERT: Absolutely, yes. Otherwise as you know, you could say a line to somebody and it could be insulting because you say it in just the wrong way. Say it a different way – just the same words – and it could be well-accepted.

Comprehension answers:
1. Without training they could not repeat performances for more than two or three nights.
2. To be able to say long sentences without pausing for breath.
3. If the thought is right.
4. They are monotonous – they drone on and on.
5. Variety. By contrasting a fast but boring motorway journey with a slower but more interesting country route.
6. Be yourself; shape the message to make it exciting; give it variety and 'build' – i.e. create a progression.
7. Variety again. Avoid being accurate but boring; study intonation in order to convey meaning without misunderstanding.

Key 2 — Food & Drink

1 **A HEALTHY DIET?**

Word power

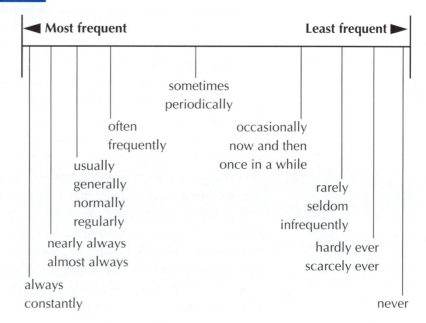

◄ Most frequent				Least frequent ►
		sometimes		
		periodically		
	often		occasionally	
	frequently		now and then	
usually			once in a while	
generally				rarely
normally				seldom
regularly				infrequently
nearly always				hardly ever
almost always				scarcely ever
always				
constantly				never

Getting it right

1. Correct.
2. Wrong. Correct version: As usual, we had chicken yesterday.
3. Correct.
4. Wrong. Correct version: We have noted a constantly increasing demand for more health foods.

2 **EATING TRENDS**

You are how you eat

Part 1

PRESENTER: Twenty years ago, when the modern eating era began, we were told that eating and our identities were inextricably linked. American gurus told us: You are what you eat. Ten years later, we

153

were constantly reminded to watch what we ate. Out went saturated fats, sugar and salt; in came fibre-rich foods, fresh fruit and
vegetables, not to mention Jane Fonda and aerobics. Having
changed our identities and our diets, the pundits are now telling us
how to eat. So, is snacking really so bad for us? Or is it simply an
excuse for the experts to have another go at us? In today's
programme, we've invited three of those very experts to give us
their views. Surely snack food doesn't need to be junk food. John?
JOHN: Of course not, Brian. And I think we need to get our defini-
tions sorted out. Junk foods are foods which contain few or even no
nutrients apart from energy.
PRESENTER: But to many listeners energy sounds positive. You seem
to be implying that it's negative.
JOHN: Well, it's easy to forget that we do need energy, or calories,
from our food. But the problem is that often we take in more calories than our body can use up. Sweets are an example of a foodstuff
with no vitamins, no minerals and no protein. Of course, they taste
delicious and are hard to resist. But the simple truth is that you
don't need sugar for energy. You get energy from all the food you
eat. Too much sugar in a diet may contribute to a general excess
energy intake, and that in turn causes obesity.
PRESENTER: So, what you're saying is that junk foods are bad for us.
JOHN: Exactly Brian. Sugary drinks, confectionery, sweets, and the
like may even lead to malnutrition. It's as serious as that.
PRESENTER: I hear approving noises around the table from our other
guests. So, agreement on that point.

Part 2
PRESENTER: OK then, so having taken junk food off the menu, are we
back with the balanced diets that were advocated ten years ago?
Diana.
DIANA: I'd like to put in a word for fast food. I think in many circles
the term has acquired a kind of derogatory meaning which I feel is
unjustified.
PRESENTER: Diana, before you put your case, can you give our
listeners a definition?
DIANA: Yes, fast food just describes snacks, perhaps one could say
substantial snacks, which are already prepared or cooked to order
within minutes so that they can be consumed on the premises or
taken away.
PRESENTER: So fast food describes both the what and the how … the

ubiquitous burger bar, the baked potato outlet and the sandwich shop being typical examples.

DIANA: Yes, exactly. Now many of the items provided by fast food outlets are of good nutritional value and totally acceptable as part of a balanced diet. This is particularly true if they are freshly cooked.

PRESENTER: Yes, Helen. Go ahead

HELEN: Thanks, Brian. But what I wanted to say is, isn't there a problem, Diana, if they are the main constituent of the diet?

DIANA: Of course, there is. But no more so than the inherent dangers of any unbalanced diet.

HELEN: I was thinking especially of the high intake of salt, energy and fat.

DIANA: I don't dispute that at all, but those same problems may be found in a non-fast food diet, too.

Part 3

PRESENTER: All right then. Can I move the discussion on to focus on snacking? And here I'd like to quote from Peter Ferguson, owner of the Healthy Snack chain, who claims 'We serve nothing but wholesome and healthy food, made from the highest quality ingredients, in a modern ambience. Our food looks good, tastes delicious and is good for you.' Now, unfortunately Peter can't be with us today, but I'd like our studio guests to respond to those claims. First, what about the principle? Helen, you're shaking your head.

HELEN: Yes, I have doubts about two aspects of Peter's claim. Firstly, I have yet to find any snack food outlet which provides a truly balanced diet and secondly ...

JOHN: I have to disagree with you there, Helen. If our main concern is simply healthy eating, then I don't see why a balanced diet can't be provided in a snack food outlet.

HELEN: John, I'm not saying it can't. But, in my experience, it simply doesn't happen. The burger culture is so firmly entrenched that it'll take a culinary revolution to replace it with something healthier.

PRESENTER: The basic problem with burgers being ...

HELEN: ... being that the meat is too fatty, as are the chips. And the bun has little nutritional value. But I really wanted to say a word about snacking. I'm very concerned about the way that snacking is changing the social aspects of eating. And I sense that we are less and less able just to sit down and eat. It's either eating and TV, or eating and work, or eating and pressure.

DIANA: But this is reflected throughout society. I don't think that eating is the only area affected.

HELEN: Oh yeah, but I see eating as a casualty of this trend. And with it, people's health. Snacking eats at the core of our well-being.

JOHN: Oh, I think you are exaggerating a little there, Helen. We live in changing times. The juggling act includes all of us with busy schedules – schoolchildren, working mothers, business people ...

HELEN: Yes, but shouldn't eating be more than just a functional activity? I mean it's surely not just a means of survival. For me snacking is really a backward step. It's food just in order to fill ...

Comprehension answers:

Part 1

Twenty years ago the modern eating era began.

Ten years later out went saturated fats, sugar and salt; in came fibre-rich foods, fresh fruit and vegetables.

Junk foods contain few or no nutrients apart from energy.

Sweets contain no vitamins, no minerals and no protein.

Part 2

Fast food describes snacks which are already prepared or cooked to order within minutes so that they can be consumed on the premises or taken away.

Three examples: burger bar, the baked potato outlet and the sandwich shop.

But fast food may result in a high intake of salt, energy and fat.

Part 3

First, Helen doubts that any snack food outlet provides a truly balanced diet.

Second, Helen is concerned about the way that snacking is changing the social aspects of eating.

Helen believes eating should be more than a functional activity.

Getting it right

1. After work I like watching television.
2. I (can) smell something strange. Is it coming from the kitchen?
3. I can recommend the restaurant. All our meals tasted good.
4. If you look over here, I'll show you something interesting.

1. I can hear footsteps. They sound like Pete's.
2. Did you get a chance to look at this report on eating habits?

3. On my way through the kitchen, by chance I saw some of their ingredients.
4. From what I saw, most of their cooking equipment looked very old-fashioned.
5. There's a gas leak; you can smell it everywhere.
6. Just listen to that noise; that food-processor needs repairing.

3 EATING CULTURES

Mind your manners!

Comprehension answers:
1. When to begin the meal, how to comment on the meal and when to apologize.
2. Always accept drinks that are offered; never start food or drink until specifically invited to do so.
3. Australia and China.

A question of style

Part 1

SPEAKER 1: If you are invited to someone's home, you may be the only guest, but that shouldn't present a problem. The British can be very hospitable. Not in an overwhelming manner, but in a typical understated way. You should take a small gift, flowers or a box of chocolates. That's always appreciated.

SPEAKER 2: In some countries it's quite common to eat with your hands – specially if you are invited to someone's house. Just remember that you absolutely mustn't touch the food with your left hand.

SPEAKER 3: Oh yes, well on a more general note, it's always a good idea to familiarize yourself with the cuisine of a country – to know what specialities to expect. And it might be a good idea to learn a few social phrases that go with table manners. It helps to lighten the atmosphere and shows that the visitor has made an effort to learn something of the culture.

Answers:
1. / 2. + 3. –

Part 2
Extract 1
A: So when are you off?
B: Next week. A direct flight to Tokyo.

A: You should try to use chopsticks. It's a gesture that's really appreciated.
B: Don't worry, I've been practising for weeks.

Extract 2
A: Well, we're planning to travel all over the country.
B: You know that here in Sweden the distances are enormous from north to south and the climate is very varied.
A: Yes, we've got a very full itinerary.
B: Anyway, when you're invited to people's homes, it's a good idea to try to eat everything on your plate.
A: Oh, really?

Extract 3
A: So, what should I do if I'm invited to someone's house? Should I take flowers?
B: Oh no. That's not necessary. If I were you, I'd just say 'thank you' as you leave. That's the way we normally do things in Canada.
A: Ah, right.

Extract 4
A: And for those of you who are intending to visit the Indian subcontinent, remember that religion plays a major role in people's lives. For example, the Hindu religion absolutely prohibits the eating of beef.

Extract 5
A: During my last visit I was invited to a number of private homes and I was never absolutely sure how to behave.
B: Well, as a rule of thumb in Saudi Arabia, you should leave soon after eating.

Extract 6
A: Although France is so close to us geographically, I always find major differences in life style and patterns of behaviour.
B: I'm surprised to hear you say that. Tell me more.
A: Well, for instance, you absolutely mustn't talk business over lunch. Meals are for cultured conversation.

Extract 7
A: I was invited to the Levy's yesterday evening.
B: How was it?

A: Very enjoyable. But I was wondering whether I should send them flowers or something?

B: No, here in Israel you ought to just send a card.

Extract 8

And for those of you going on to Malaysia, a word of advice. Remember that it is forbidden for Muslims to drink alcohol. So, if you're invited out, you absolutely mustn't take any alcohol as a gift.

Country	Do/Don't	Strength
Canada	Say thank you as you leave	–
France	Talk business over lunch	+
India	Assume Hindus eat beef	+
Israel	Send a thank you card	/
Japan	Try to use chopsticks	/
Malaysia	Bring alcoholic drinks	+
Saudi Arabia	Leave soon after eating	/
Sweden	Eat everything on your plate	–

4   DRINKING PATTERNS

 New wines for old?

Part 1

INTERVIEWER: Steven, could you tell us a bit about where the wines you produce come from exactly?

STEVEN BURNS: Well California is almost as large as the country of France. It's more than one thousand miles long and I've heard that they grow wine grapes from one end of California to the other. Napa Valley I think many people have heard of and it's – although it accounts for only 17 per cent of California's wine – it's one of the most famous wine producing areas in the world.

INTERVIEWER: Any other geographical areas ?

STEVEN BURNS: There, well, unfortunately there are 52 designated approved viticultural areas, which is this crazy thing that we have where we try to identify the different soil types and micro-climates that exist in California for wine production.

INTERVIEWER: Right, and what about the actual features of the most popular wines that you produce? Can you characterize them?

STEVEN BURNS: Well I know some people in the wine industry tend to categorize California as (a) new world wine producer, but actually they've been making and producing grape wine in California even before there was a California and we do have our native grape. It's called Zinfandel and you can find Zinfandel in most grocery stores and supermarkets around the world these days.

INTERVIEWER: Just a minute Steven – Zinfandel – how do you spell that?

STEVEN BURNS: Well it's z-i-n-f-a-n-d-e-l. And what we say in California is, 'Life is hell without Zinfandel.'

INTERVIEWER: What about the flavour of it, is it a particular style, is it light, heavy?

STEVEN BURNS: Well that's the fun thing about Zinfandel – [is] it's an adaptable red grape. You can make it in a white light rosé style that works very well in California when the temperatures get warm. Also it's a very serious red wine grape that makes very excellent red wines that you can lay down for decades almost.

INTERVIEWER: So would you say that California's producing classic wines or are they more popular, everyday sort of wines?

STEVEN BURNS: Well California invented the varietal concept for naming wines. We were the first people to name wines Chardonnay, after the grape that actually goes in the bottle, so we like to think that we put the fun back in wine drinking, but we also do make some very serious wines that can be compared with the best wines of Bordeaux.

Part 2

INTERVIEWER: What about the main markets for the wines you produce?

STEVEN BURNS: Well, our largest export market is our neighbour to the north, Canada, and of course our second largest market is the United Kingdom. Our growth markets are Denmark, Germany, Singapore, Hong Kong and Mexico – surprisingly enough, it's a large growing market for food and drink of all kind of styles.

INTERVIEWER: So these are the trends you would see in the actual export market … moving more away from traditional wine drinking markets to new ones?

STEVEN BURNS: Well we hope that's the case. I think that people are enjoying wine more and more with their meals; they're drinking less and less of spirits and more expensive beverages and really enjoying their wines, particularly the red wines. We've been doing some research on wine as part of a healthy diet, and in fact red wine is supposed to be very – 'heart-healthy' is the words we like to use in California.

INTERVIEWER: Heart-healthy?

STEVEN BURNS: Yep, and you can even see bumper stickers when you're driving around California: 'Treat your heart to a glass of red wine today.' So we – we like to look for any excuse to enjoy ourselves in California – we kind of live up to our lifestyle, but basically our wine is exported to most countries around the world.

INTERVIEWER: Right. Steven, you were talking about wine being heart-healthy; can we talk a bit more about that? I mean is wine perceived as being a healthy or a dangerous thing in different parts of the world?

STEVEN BURNS: I think in general alcohol has been perceived as something that's not positive; it's not a healthy thing to include in your diet, but about fifteen years ago some significant research was being done comparing the American diet and the French diet and, as we all know, if anybody's travelled to France they know that the diet is … very high in saturated fats and butters and cheeses and yet the heart disease rate in France is one tenth of that … that exists in America and what they attributed that to was the moderate consumption over the long term of red wine.

INTERVIEWER: And what did they reckon was a sort of reasonable consumption of red wine?

STEVEN BURNS: That's the problem, 'reasonable' they defined as one to two glasses a day, and it really was a way to clean out your arteries of unhealthy fatty deposits and so we've seen in the last year a consumption of red wine in California particularly increase, more than 60 per cent.

Part 3

INTERVIEWER: And finally Steven, can you tell us something about some of the recent trends in wine drinking and what you think some future trends might be?

STEVEN BURNS: Well that's anybody's guess but the most interesting thing about overall alcohol consumption these days is it's down. But wine consumption is up around the world and even established wine drinkers that have been drinking wine for years are drinking better wines and so, so they're less satisfied with basic table wines and people are purchasing varietal wines and vintage dated wines and (are) really willing to pay that extra amount of money to get a better quality product 'cause they realize they enjoy it that much more.

INTERVIEWER: So you're saying that although this is all over the world, the actual consumption of alcohol all over the world is down, wine itself is going up in the world?

STEVEN BURNS: Wine consumption is rising considerably and it's a –

it's a combination of things, I think that one of the things that I hope California is do – has done is take the mystery out of wine and by using the varietal concept Chardonnay, Cabernet, all those words that we're all familiar with these days. So what we've done – after the varietal concept, is, California's done a lot of research on producing organic wines. We think that that's a part of the global living in the nineties, and in the next century that we'll require wine producers all around the world to make more environmentally friendly products, and that means organically produced grapes, not using lead in their foils, recycling bottles, producing alcohol-free wines for those countries or consumers that don't wish to, to consume alcohol but would like to enjoy wines with their meals.

INTERVIEWER: Any other trends for the future?

STEVEN BURNS: Well I think that wine is going to be considered a food in the years ahead, I think that's a –

INTERVIEWER: A food!

STEVEN BURNS: – that's a concept and it's going to be enjoyed mostly with meals and we're going to look at our wine selection as we do (ask ourselves), are we going to have beef or chicken or are we going to have – what kind of vegetable – tonight, and we strongly believe that wine is a lifestyle beverage and that it is a choice of what kind of water you'll have or what kind of wine you'll have, and that it will become an integrated part of global society as it is in France, as it is in California these days.

Comprehension answers:

Part 1

Area of wine production: One end of California to the other; Napa valley; 52 designated areas.

Features of the wines: New World; zinfandel grape; adaptable; varietal concept; fun and serious wines.

Slogan for Zinfandel: 'Life is hell without Zinfandel.'

Part 2

Main export markets for the wines: Canada, UK, Denmark, Germany, Singapore, Hong Kong, Mexico.

Recent changes in drinking habits and attitudes: More wines with meals; less spirits; moderate consumption of red wines now thought to be healthy.

Slogan for red wine: Either 'heart healthy' or 'treat your heart to a glass of red wine today.'

Part 3

World-wide trends in drinking habits: Alcohol consumption down overall, yet wine drinking up; varietal wines up; more organic wines; more alcohol-free wines; wines will be considered a food – with meals.

Slogan for wine 'as a beverage': 'Wine is a lifestyle beverage'.

A question of style

Several combinations are possible, but we would suggest the following:

1. (c) I'm sorry, but dinner will be a bit late.
2. (f) I really must apologize for missing that meeting. You see, I was caught in the traffic downtown.
3. (a) I'm afraid I've got some really bad news for you. You see just as Tiddles was coming out of the driveway ...
4. (b) Well, unfortunately, just as I was going to set off ...
5. (d) I'm sorry to have to tell you that I can't make our meeting after all.
6. (e) I regret to inform you that your application was unsuccessful.

The World of Work

Key 3

1   PROFILES

Word power

1. (d, h, p)   2. (e, k, w)   3. (g, u, v)   4.(a, j, q)
5. (i, m, t)   6. (b, n, x)   7. (c, o, s)   8. (f, l, r)

2   TOO MUCH WORK?

The overworked society

Comprehension answers:
The three groups are: the structurally unemployed; the insecure self-employed; the core elite.

Word power

1. The workforce is underemployed. They spend half the day sitting around doing nothing.
2. I'm afraid he's unemployable. He's got no qualifications, no experience, and no motivation.
3. Most people used to think that being an employee was much more secure than being self-employed.
4. Overemployment is a relatively new phenomenon, brought on by companies reducing the number of employees to a bare minimum.
5. Employers should think carefully before cutting their work-forces.

3   WOMEN'S WORK

Equal or better?

 Part 1

INTERVIEWER: Catherine, would you say that as a woman it's been more difficult for you to climb the corporate ladder?
CATHERINE PERRY: Not necessarily. In the early stages of my career the progress was relatively smooth. I think if you have the required training and experience, and you're willing to devote yourself to

getting ahead, that you can do so quite easily. The difficulties occur later, the competition gets tougher and your personal life may be more demanding, especially if you're trying to combine your career with a family.

INTERVIEWER: Do you think there's more resentment from your male colleagues, the higher up the ladder you get?

CATHERINE PERRY: No, I don't think it's necessarily the resentment from male colleagues – it could well be females who have made it and had to pay a dear price for that, and I think it just has to do with general attitudes and culture.

INTERVIEWER: I read a recent report which said that women are actually opting out of management careers in ever increasing numbers. Why do you think this would be so?

CATHERINE PERRY: Well, I think women, and some men as well, are opting out of management careers because they often become too demanding and stressful, not necessarily intellectually but emotionally and even physically. Corporate politics is usually to blame for that fact.

INTERVIEWER: In what sense?

CATHERINE PERRY: Well management jobs tend to try to absorb the total person, and they demand time far beyond what should be required to succeed in a career – and I think there are lots of other career options that give you the intellectual stimulation, give you more time and flexibility, you can still earn good money and basically, there's no wonder people are leaving management.

INTERVIEWER: Right. Can you give us some examples of these alternatives?

CATHERINE PERRY: Well I think once you've reached a certain point in your career, let's say you've been a director of a company, it's very easy to then go into consulting. You have a broad base of experience, maybe experience in different industries.

Part 2

INTERVIEWER: So you become freelance, you work from a small office or from home, and your life changes in that way, is that necessarily a good thing?

CATHERINE PERRY: Well it can be for many people and certainly working from home or a small office often suits some people but for other people, they're used to having a very corporate surrounding, they like lots of human interaction and there are other choices, and oftentimes companies will bring freelance people in and allow them to work in there full time and only tap into their services when they need them and the rest of the time they can get on with their other work.

INTERVIEWER: So Catherine, do you think there's a particular advantage for women following this line of being freelance and working from home?

CATHERINE PERRY: Well I think it can be very advantageous for women depending on their lifestyle – combining their work with their family. I think it works very well.

Part 3

INTERVIEWER: To what extent do you think that corporations and businesses play their part in supporting women when they have children, when they probably need more time off? Do you think they're doing their bit?

CATHERINE PERRY: No, I think they're doing absolutely nothing. And not only are they not supporting women, they're discriminating against women that have children. Subsequently they're discriminating against families, and men as well suffer in the process.

INTERVIEWER: I mean, on a general point, do you think it's still true that women are paid less than men?

CATHERINE PERRY: I think I'd have to say yes, there's been a lot of … a lot of statistics that have come out about that, but I think companies often rationalize about why that's the case but I'm afraid it's still – it still is true.

INTERVIEWER: On the popularity of certain jobs do you think women are sort of more suited for certain jobs than other jobs, or is everything equal?

CATHERINE PERRY: Well it seems to be the case that some professions do lend themselves, and certainly where physical strength is involved, most women are typically smaller and not as strong as men. Other professions – there seems to be more women in them for whatever reason and they do well in it, and that encourages women to continue to join those professions.

INTERVIEWER: Professions like what?

CATHERINE PERRY: Oh like public relations and teaching, nursing, I think public service work.

INTERVIEWER: Do you think there are any sort of special skills or intuitions that women have that they can bring to business that men don't have? Are there sort of special gifts that women have and should exploit?

CATHERINE PERRY: I think there's a lot of talk about that, but I think really it's about people and whether you're male or female – we all have different strengths and weaknesses – we're all different personality types and I suppose there should be less focus about the actual sex of the person and more on what they actually bring to the party as an individual.

Comprehension answers:
1. '… and you're willing to devote yourself to getting ahead.'
2. ' … your personal life gets more demanding.'
3.. 'Management jobs tend to try to absorb the total person.'
4. '… other people are used to having a very corporate surrounding, they like lots of human interaction.'
5. 'I think it can be very advantageous for women, depending on their lifestyle … combining work and their family.'
6. '… not only are they not supporting women, they're discriminating against women that have children.'
7. '… companies often rationalize about why that's the case.'
8. 'There should be less focus about the actual sex of the person and more on what they actually bring to the party as an individual.'

4   WHAT'S YOUR LINE?

Jobs and career moves

Interview 1
INTERVIEWER: François, what do you for a living?
FRANÇOIS: I'm a software engineer.
INTERVIEWER: And is that something you always wanted to do?
FRANÇOIS: Well, I've always been into computers, you know.
INTERVIEWER: So you looked for something in that line?
FRANÇOIS: Yes, I suppose so. I studied IT at university.
INTERVIEWER: IT – that stands for Information Technology, I guess?
FRANÇOIS: That's right.
INTERVIEWER: And has the work turned out to be what you expected?
FRANÇOIS: Well, it's OK. We're a bit cut off from the rest of the world, if you know what I mean .... I reckon I might look around for something a bit more mainstream.
INTERVIEWER: So, what would you see as mainstream?
FRANÇOIS: Well, I might move into the marketing side. It's got a bit more life to it.

Interview 2

INTERVIEWER: Petra, what sort of job do you have?

PETRA: To be honest, I don't have a job at the moment.

INTERVIEWER: Did you lose your job, then?

PETRA: No, I stopped working about six years ago to look after my children.

INTERVIEWER: I see, so how long have you been looking for a job?

PETRA: About six months.

INTERVIEWER: And what sort of job are you after?

PETRA: Well, I trained as a dental technician, so I'd like to get back into that type of work ... you know, work with a dentist or at a hospital.

INTERVIEWER: And you're finding it tough to find a job?

PETRA: It certainly is. I don't think my age helps – you know they want to take on young technicians who have just recently qualified.

INTERVIEWER: So what's your next move?

PETRA: I think I'm going to have to look further afield … you know, maybe try other towns and cities.

INTERVIEWER: That's going to cause problems, isn't it?

PETRA: Of course, but what choice do I have?

Interview 3

INTERVIEWER: Carlos, how many jobs have you had?

CARLOS: At the last count, I think it was 24!

INTERVIEWER: That's a lot of employers. Have you always worked in the same line?

CARLOS: Oh yes, always in sales.

INTERVIEWER: And how come you have moved around so much?

CARLOS: Oh, I don't know. There was always a good reason. You know, better money, more opportunities …

INTERVIEWER: I see, so how long have you been working?

CARLOS: Since I was 16 ... so that's 31 years. I remember my first job … I started out as an ice-cream boy at the local football stadium …

INTERVIEWER: So what's your line now?

CARLOS: Well, time's are hard – there's not many jobs around – so I'm thinking of starting up on my own.

INTERVIEWER: What sort of business are you going after?

CARLOS: I reckon there's a great market helping all these small companies to sell – you know that's what I'm good at. I'm sure I've got something to offer.

Interview 4

INTERVIEWER: Matthew, I believe you've just finished your studies. Have you got a job?

MATTHEW: Yes, I've got a job ... not much of one though.

INTERVIEWER: So what are you doing?

MATTHEW: I'm working in a bar serving drinks.

INTERVIEWER: And what did you study?

MATTHEW: I studied physics.

INTERVIEWER: Well I thought that was what we needed ... you know more scientists and all that?

MATTHEW: That's what they told me too when I was at school.

INTERVIEWER: So what's the difficulty ... are there just no jobs?

MATTHEW: Well, I'd like to work in research –

INTERVIEWER: Yes?

MATTHEW: – but it seems most companies are cutting back on research at the moment.

INTERVIEWER: So, what's your next step?

MATTHEW: I'm going to try to work abroad ... at least that way I'll get some useful experience.

INTERVIEWER: Have you had any offers?

MATTHEW: Yeah, actually I've just heard from a firm in Hamburg – they might take me on as a market researcher.

INTERVIEWER: But that's not really what you had in mind, is it?

MATTHEW: No, but beggars can't be choosers.

Interviewees	Job/profession	Current problems	Next step
François Bergerac	Software engineer	Too cut off	Looking for job in marketing
Petra Telleman	Dental technician	Unemployed	Try further afield
Carlos Rodrigues	Salesman	Business is tough	Start up own business
Matthew Tate	Barman	Wants a job in scientific research	Job in Hamburg

Getting it right

1. The new job turned out much better than expected.
2. The company has cut back on all areas of expenditure.
3. I'm afraid he's after my job, but he's not going to get it.
4. I had to turn down the job despite the good salary.
5. They aren't taking on any new recruits.

6. She had to stop work to look after her children.
7. Don't worry. I'm sure something will turn up.
8. He gets on really well with his boss.
9. It's never worth making it up. It's better to tell the truth.
10. I don't think this job is going to come off. It looks as if they're going to appoint someone internally.

Key 4 Travel

A question of style

Advice for travellers

1. (1) ship   (2) plane   (3) car   (4) camel   (5) bicycle   (6) train

2. Vocabulary features: (1) watery death; (4) species; (6) posture

Structural features: (4) the construction with 'should' is today only used in formal language, e.g. legal contracts.

Information: (6) The advice to remain in your place on a train seems old-fashioned.

3. Model answer: Nothing is more tiring than the back-breaking monotonous swing of this creature. And, if the rider loses patience and gives the animal a sharp crack of the whip to make it trot, the torture is like having your spine driven by a sledge-hammer from below, half a foot deeper into your skull.

Word power

relations: grandfather, father, uncle
bones: spine, skull
weather conditions: wet, foggy, windy, icy
hazards/dangers: mud, gravel, snow

The following are examples only; others are possible.
creature: horse, dog, bird, insect
clothing: shirt, trousers, jumper, shoes
colour: red, orange, yellow, green, brown, indigo, violet
two-wheeler: bike/bicycle, motor-cycle

Getting it right

1. Items may have moved because of/owing to/due to turbulent conditions in the air.
2. As/Because/Since take-off and landing are dangerous, you must keep your seat belts fastened.

3. A combination of bad weather and poor driving causes/leads to many road accidents.
4. You could easily slip and injure yourself. Therefore, never try to jump onto a moving train.
5. Due to/Because of/Owing to bad weather conditions, there have been many delays throughout southeast Asia.

2   LINGUA TOURISTICA

Signs to remember?

Model answers:
Japanese hotel: Your chambermaid will be happy to help you.
Swiss restaurant: Our wines leave nothing to be desired.
Tailor's shop in Hong Kong: Gentlemen's fitting room upstairs.
Swedish fur shop: Ladies fur coats made up. Bring your own material.
Tailor's shop in Nairobi: Order your summer suit. Because of the heavy demand we will execute orders in strict rotation.
Copenhagen airport: We can send your bags to any destination required.
Norwegian cocktail bar: Ladies are requested not to bring children into the bar.
Budapest zoo: Please do not feed the animals. Donations of food can be left with the keeper on duty.
Beijing doctor's surgery: Specialist in women's and other diseases
Tokyo hotel: Please do not remove the hotel towels.

3   MIXED BLESSINGS

Tourism: For and against

INTERVIEWER: First we hear from a restaurant owner in Italy … Are you affected by tourism?
RESTAURANT OWNER: Absolutely. We depend on tourists. They are tremendously important to our business and to the local economy. Fortunately, the holiday season is getting longer and longer. Unfortunately, visitors today spend less.
INTERVIEWER: Why is that?
RESTAURANT OWNER: I think tourists coming here are now more careful with their money; it has to go further. Tourists used to spend a lot of money on meals and drinks; now they have to be more economical.

INTERVIEWER: And do you see any problems with tourism?

RESTAURANT OWNER: As far as I am concerned I see no special problems caused by visitors. In a large city there are always problems. And we are used to hearing about street violence, breathing in traffic fumes, and seeing rubbish. But it would be wrong to blame the tourists for these.

INTERVIEWER: Now we move to Spain and hear from a local farmer …

FARMER: These people come tramping across our land. They have no respect for other people's property – especially those that come from the cities. They think that because it's in the countryside, it belongs to everyone. They don't seem to realize that my land is like their houses. I don't go into their houses without permission; they shouldn't come onto my land. What do they say in England? An Englishman's home is his castle. It's the same with my land. It's very simple; the walls are there to keep people out, whether it be from their houses or from my land. But they just don't take any notice. I want to work my land and not be disturbed by visitors. That's how we've lived for hundreds of years. I don't see any reason for changing our way of life now. And that's what tourism does – it disturbs me and changes the way we live.

On to Tobago, where we speak to a local islander …

INTERVIEWER: This is a very picturesque part of the world and one which the guidebooks all mention. So this must draw a lot of tourists.

ISLANDER: Yes, we've seen major changes in our island since tourists arrived in large numbers. But we're getting used to seeing them now. It's not a bad thing, as far as I'm concerned.

INTERVIEWER: I'm surprised that you should feel so positive about them.

ISLANDER: Well, I used to object to them. You know, the crowds and the noise. But I've got used to them now. All in all, I think they've been a benefit to the community.

INTERVIEWER: In what way?

ISLANDER: Firstly, cultural. People come from all over to visit us. And they give us a window on the world. It means that we're no longer a backwater, no longer so isolated. Of course, not everybody would agree; some of the locals would prefer them not to come, would like to preserve island life as it was years ago. But, I don't think you can turn back the clocks; I'm all for progress. And then of course, there's the financial side. Visitors spend money here. And that's good for everyone.

Now we hear from a backpacker walking in the mountains of Nepal …

BACKPACKER: It's absolutely wonderful – this sense of total freedom. Just take a look at the views of these mountains. It's totally unique. And the villages are just so unspoilt.

INTERVIEWER: But don't you think that you and all the backpackers walking in the Himalayas may be spoiling it?

BACKPACKER: Why should we be spoiling it? All we're doing is walking and enjoying the scenery. Surely that isn't doing any harm?

INTERVIEWER: Yes, but don't you think that you are having an impact on the lives of the villagers? They bring up Coca Cola on donkeys just for you; it's part of your lifestyle – not theirs. And that is one example of how you're changing their lives.

BACKPACKER: But their lives are changing anyway. In the last village I stayed, they've now got electricity. You can't imagine how delighted they are. Just think of all the things they can now do. You can't isolate these people just so that we can show them off as museum pieces. Progress will come anyway. Tourism puts some money in their pockets so they can enjoy progress.

INTERVIEWER: Distant Dreams organizes tours to holiday destinations throughout the world. Their sales director talks to us now.

SALES DIRECTOR: Tourism is part of the leisure industry, which is one of the fastest growing sectors in our country. People have more and more time on their hands; they want to explore more and more of our planet. Now people come in all shapes and sizes and they want different types of holidays. And our job is to respond to that need, be it a beach holiday, a safari holiday, walking, a city break, visiting antiquities, whatever. We are guided by the market.

INTERVIEWER: And how do you see the effects of what you're doing?

SALES DIRECTOR: It has two sides. We give the tourist the package that he or she wants. We make their dreams come true – that's the service we provide, the benefit to the customer. We also play a significant role in a number of local economies. The domestic one comes first, where we employ some 250 people. Then there are the destinations in our brochure. And naturally tourism has a major impact there too – providing jobs throughout the sector – hotels, restaurants, shops, etc. Our philosophy in Distant Dreams is: People work hard for 45-odd weeks of the year. They deserve the break that they want. That's their reward. And if their wish is to lie on a beach, fringed with palm trees, with waitresses dancing in grass skirts, then we'll give it to them.

Speaker	For tourism	Against tourism	Benefits	Drawbacks
Restaurant owner	✓		business, local economy	–
Local farmer		✓	–	visitors disturb land, privacy and lifestyle
Islander	✓		cultural window on the world; visitors spend money	crowds, noise
Backpacker	✓		tourist's sense of freedom; villagers can enjoy economic benefits of progress	–
Tour operator	✓		makes customers' dreams come true; jobs for local economies	–

Getting it right

1. The British travel abroad a lot, so they are used to driving on the right.
2. In the past visitors to our restaurant used to spend a lot more on food and drink than they do today.
3. People working in the catering business are used to working long hours, even today.
4. As they lived on a very remote farm, they were not used to seeing many people.
5. We expect that the number of visitors will increase; and many of those visitors will be used to receiving a high level of personal service.
6. In the old days travellers used to have to put up with a lot of discomfort.

A question of style

CUSTOMER: We're looking for a holiday by the seaside.

AGENT: Do you (*spoken:* d'you) have anywhere particular in mind?

CUSTOMER: We've never been to Greece. So that would (*spoken:* that'd) be one possibility.

AGENT: Just a minute and I'll check our catalogues. Yes, here's one on the island of Corfu. Last week you'd have (*spoken:* you'd've) paid double for this holiday. This week it's on special offer. Clients who've been there have been very pleased. The hotel accommodation's right on the beach. I don't think there are many places left. I'll just check.

4 A BAD IMAGE

'If only they'd stay at home'

Part 1

INTERVIEWER: Alistair, we've read a lot in the newspapers about skirmishes and fights involving holidaymakers from Albion to the Alcoste, getting drunk, smashing things up. How big a problem is this exactly?

ALISTAIR PARKER: Well, actually it's a very small problem. It's certainly embarrassing for us, but it's blown up out of all proportion by the popular press, by the tabloid newspapers.

INTERVIEWER: I see. And who exactly is responsible for all these – ?

ALISTAIR PARKER: Oh only very small elements of our holidaymakers. Some have a few drinks too many and lose control, get into brawls. And this … creates a bad image for – for all the visitors here from our country.

INTERVIEWER: But isn't this really a problem for the Alcoste authorities, not for you?

ALISTAIR PARKER: No, it's a problem for us and for them. We need to maintain good relations with the authorities so that they welcome our bona fide tourists. We must also show the local authorities that we're – we're doing our bit at home to combat the problem.

INTERVIEWER: Mm.

ALISTAIR PARKER: So we try to get these people sent back rather than face criminal proceedings here.

INTERVIEWER: Oh I see – they're sent back home rather than go on trial actually in the Alcoste?

ALISTAIR PARKER: Oh yes, yes, yes. We deal very harshly with these hooligans. Firstly, we're – we're working with the travel agencies back home so that they promote our message that troublemakers will be sent home.

INTERVIEWER: Mm.

ALISTAIR PARKER: Secondly, we work with the hotels, restaurants and bars here, assuring them that we deal harshly with our own people.

Thirdly, we liaise with the local police to ensure that these vandals are repatriated straight away.

INTERVIEWER: I see, right.

[Handwritten margin notes:]
- 2 other words for fights
- who exaggerated these stories.
- large % of holiday makers.
- who is it a problem for
- what does Alistair try to do with the people who cause problems. Rather than what?
- What are they doing ... back home + abroad.
1.
2.
3.

Part 2

INTERVIEWER: I see, and what about the costs of this operation of sending them home? Who – who pays for all this?

ALISTAIR PARKER: Oh well, of course there is a cost, but – but we consider it's money well spent, to prevent trouble and to promote the image of our country. We don't want to be seen as ignoring the problem nor as exporting it and … shirking our responsibility.

INTERVIEWER: No, I see that, but is it in fact the Albion taxpayer who has to foot the bill for all this?

ALISTAIR PARKER: No, no, no. It's shared out between the authorities here, and various agencies and organizations back home.

INTERVIEWER: Oh I see.

ALISTAIR PARKER: And of course, if a troublemaker is repatriated, they get a pretty hefty bill, I can tell you, and we get the money back from him or her.

INTERVIEWER: Oh I see. So the people you send back home, they actually have to pay to be sent back home, is that …?

ALISTAIR PARKER: Absolutely, yes.

INTERVIEWER: Well I – that all seems very draconian, doesn't it? I mean, aren't you being a bit harsh? Surely it's not a – you know, it's not only the Albion tourists that get out of hand and create a problem, is it?

ALISTAIR PARKER: Yes, but I don't think one can be too harsh with these people. We feel that we have a responsibility to the host community here in the Alcoste and, in any case, let me reassure you that we're only talking about a very small handful of people who get into trouble. And, as I've said before, it's just the newspapers who enjoy blowing up these types of stories. They get out of all proportion.

Comprehension answers:

1. the popular press, the tabloid newspapers
2. creates a bad image
3. doing our bit; to combat the problem
4. these vandals are repatriated
5. money well spent
6. shirking our responsibility
7. actually have to pay
8. responsibility to the host community

Word power

1. No, actually it's brown. / Well actually I bought a brown one.
2. Yes, it's really excellent.
3. Well, actually, yes I have.
4. Yes, it's really awful.

Key 5 Education

1 SCHOOL OF LIFE

Getting it right

1. Since no one would help him, he had to do it by himself.
2. Given the right environment, children are quite capable of learning by themselves.
3. In a kindergarten or nursery school children are encouraged to play with one another.
4. Twins are a very special case since they are often very supportive of each other.
5. My brother and I supported ourselves during our university studies.
6. If you don't succeed, you will have only yourself/yourselves to blame.

2 DEAR EDITOR

Letter from a headmaster

Comprehension answers:

1. To hire and fire teachers; to admit and expel pupils
2. Changing the traditional relationship between teacher and pupils makes the pupils disoriented.
3. The personal style invites personal contact; the impersonal style rejects it.

Word power

spate (c) shortage	advocate (c) discourage
benefit (d) disadvantage	flourish (a) wither

democracy	autocracy
liberal	conservative
confusion	order
former	latter
virtues	vices

A question of style

Part 1: Dialogue 1
First we hear from two parents:

MRS BROWN: Well, I think that standards of discipline in school and in the classroom have declined significantly over the last few years. I've heard from my son Peter some of the things that go on in his class and quite frankly I am shocked. Things are getting out of hand. I reckon it's education that needs tightening up.

OTHER PARENT: I totally agree with you. If you can't get discipline right in the classroom, what chance do the children have? Pick up a newspaper. All you read about are increased levels of violence on our streets.

Dialogue 2
Next we hear a concerned parent talking to a headteacher:

MRS BROWN: And quite frankly, I'm concerned about standards of discipline in this school. I have heard from my son Peter of some of the things that go on in his class and, to tell you the truth, I'm shocked. It seems that teachers today just can't keep order.

HEAD: Well, Mrs Brown. I really can't accept your generalization about bad behaviour in the classroom. Of course it's natural for parents to be anxious about discipline. There's nothing wrong with that. Except that I think there's a tendency for people to overreact and attack schools whenever they're worried about society.

Dialogue 3
Next we hear two teachers discussing a pupil:

TEACHER 1: That Peter Brown is heading for trouble. His work is atrociously presented and his attitude is totally negative. And the effect he has on others! When he's away, the class is no trouble at all. When he's there, it's one annoyance after another. I think it's time to have words with the head.

TEACHER 2: To a certain extent, I agree that he is a trouble-maker. But let me give you a little advice. I have been a teacher for twenty years now and I have never known a class without one Peter Brown. It's just a question of wills: yours against his. I'm sure that if you establish a little more authority in class, he'll come to respect you. And then you'll see his work'll improve.

Answers:
1. +   2. −   3. /

Part 2: Extracts 1-8

1. A: Teachers already receive a reasonable salary for the work they do. I mean, what other profession gets such long holidays a year?
B: I'm afraid I can't accept that teachers are well paid. In fact, for the hours they put in, their pay is less than a skilled manual worker.
2. A: Listen, what we need is not more teachers, but better teachers. If we want to streamline the profession, then we should be looking for quality.
B: Up to a point I'd agree with you, but if we cut back too far, then we increase class sizes and that is not in the pupils' interests.
3. A: Poor discipline in the classroom is directly linked to the increased levels of crime in society.
B: To a certain extent I'd accept that, but it's an oversimplification to link all delinquency to poor classroom discipline.
4. A: Children should be given more responsibility in the running of the school.
B: I'm all in favour of that. That's the way to help them to become more reliable adults.
5. A: Education is becoming far too specialized at a young age. Of course, I know that we need experts for our future needs, but school should give pupils a basis for life.
B: Up to a point, I'd accept that, but on the other hand, if we wait too long before identifying potential expertise, we could be wasting opportunities.
6. A: Every child is good at something. It's up to the school to find his strengths and develop them.
B: I totally agree with you. And you've put your finger on the key. Finding potential is what education should be about.
7. A: There's far too much pressure on kids in school today. Pressure to get on, to be successful. Where's the fun?
B: I can't go along with you on that. For the majority of kids, school still provides an interesting and enjoyable environment.
8. A: I think that teachers should have a dose of their own medicine. Go back to school for a week or a month. Find out what it's like to be stuck in school all day, listening to boring lessons.
B: Yeah, well, you may have something there, but I'm not sure it'll do much to change the system.

Agreement: 4 and 6.
Partial agreement: 2, 3, 5 and 8.
Disagreement: 1 and 7.

Sound advice

*auto*crat – au*to*cracy
res*pon*sible – responsi*bili*ty
main*tain* – *main*tenance
au*thori*ty – *autho*rize
*recog*nize – recog*nition*
*ope*rate – oper*ation*

Word check

aristocracy: rule by the best individuals of a relatively small privileged class
bureaucracy: rule by administrators
plutocracy: rule by the rich
technocracy: rule by the technical specialists

3   CAMPUS ORIGINS

Getting started

Oxford, UK; Montpellier, France; Cordoba, Argentina; Prague, the Czech Republic; Heidelberg, Germany; Stanford, USA; Nihon, Japan; Witwatersrand, South Africa.

A comparative survey

Part 1
FRANK: OK guys, let's get started, OK? We've got to report back in about an hour. How about going round the table to see what we all got?
BRIGITTE: It might be more efficient if one of us took notes so that we've got a record of the main points.
MANUEL: Good proposal. We have to write a brief report anyway. I suggest that we write the principal points down immediately.
FRANK: Alberto, what do you say to that?
ALBERTO: I agree. If you want, I'll take notes.
FRANK: Thanks for volunteering, Alberto. Anyway, your handwriting's bound to be more legible than mine. OK, who's going to start? Manuel, you've got an awesome pile of papers in front of you. Remember, we've only got a limited time.
MANUEL: OK, I'll start. Alberto, are you ready for a little information about Spain?
ALBERTO: Yes.
MANUEL: So, the oldest university that I've discovered is the University of Salamanca.
FRANK: Sounds like an animal to me.

MANUEL: Very funny, Frank. Ha, ha, ha. So, it was founded in … Oh yes. I've got a bit of a problem here, because I found two dates. It appears that Alfonso IX established it in 1218, but it was his grandson Alfonso X who really started it in 1254.

BRIGITTE: And who were these Alfonsos?

MANUEL: Kings of Spain.

ALBERTO: Right, I have noted all that.

BRIGITTE: And what was on offer?

MANUEL: Well, the students could study law, grammar, arts and physics.

FRANK: Does it still exist today?

MANUEL: Oh yes, it certainly does. It's been through various stages. 'The university was at its peak in 1584, when it had almost 7,000 students. Then it went into decline and by 1875 enrollment was down to just 391. Today it has about 24,000 students.' Is that enough?

FRANK: For now, yes. Brigitte, how about Germany?

Part 2

FRANK: Brigitte, how about Germany?

BRIGITTE: Well, I've got some information about Heidelberg.

ALBERTO: Excuse me, Brigitte. Is that with b-e-r-g or b-u-r-g?

BRIGITTE: B-e-r-g, berg as in mountain. You can see it here on the map – in southwestern Germany. So, I found out the following. The university was established in 1389. And the first college was a religious college belonging to the Cistercian order.

MANUEL: So, only religious instruction?

BRIGITTE: Yes, and a very strict lifestyle.

ALBERTO: What do you mean?

BRIGITTE: Well, the Cistercians believed in silence, prayer and lots of hard physical work.

FRANK: Doesn't sound like a lot of fun to me.

BRIGITTE: Well, the following year, that's 1390, a secular college was established and that would have taught similar subjects to Salamanca – science, law, philosophy and the arts.

ALBERTO: OK, I've got that. And, anything about the size?

BRIGITTE: In the fourteenth century, I couldn't find anything. Today, there are about 30,000 students there. That's all.

FRANK: Good, how about Alberto next?

Part 3

FRANK: Good, how about Alberto next?

ALBERTO: OK. Frank, why don't you take notes while I'm speaking?

FRANK: If you insist. Remember, I warned you about my writing.

BRIGITTE: Just do your best, Frank.

ALBERTO: OK, I have found out a little about our oldest university in Italy. It is named the University of Bologna. It is located here just north of the centre of Italy. And in fact some people say that Bologna is the oldest university in Europe. So old that I haven't got a precise date for its foundation. The book just says 'in the 11th century'.

FRANK: OK, I've got that. And what was it famous for?

ALBERTO: Well, apparently it was renowned all over Europe as a principal centre for juridical – juridical studies?

FRANK: Ah, juridical?

ALBERTO: Yes, juridical. The study of law.

FRANK: OK. Anything else?

ALBERTO: Yes, I said before that the university developed as a centre for law studies. Well, the first students were mostly mature men who were working in various departments either of the church or of the state.

FRANK: Fine, that just leaves the United States. Well, as you can imagine, we have to jump a few centuries till we get to our first university, Harvard. In fact it wasn't even called a university at first, but a college.

BRIGITTE: I suppose we're talking about the 17th century here.

FRANK: Yes, 1636 to be precise. It's in Cambridge which is just west of Boston, here.

MANUEL: Yes, OK.

ALBERTO: Yes right. And was there a Mr Harvard?

FRANK: Yes, exactly. A Mr John Harvard, who left all his books to the college as well as half his estate.

BRIGITTE: Very generous of him.

FRANK: He was a Puritan minister and the college started off under church sponsorship. But it gradually added other courses of instruction in law, medicine, as well as divinity.

MANUEL: I seem to remember that it has educated a few US presidents.

FRANK: Yes, six so far, including JFK.

BRIGITTE: Oh, have any of you seen the film?

MANUEL: Yes, I have …

Country	University	Founded	Other information
Spain	Salamanca	1218 or 1254	Studies in law, grammar, arts, physics; 1584 – 7,000 students; 1875 – 391 students; today – about 24,000 students.
Germany	Heidelberg	1389	Religious college belonging to the Cistercian order; 1390 – a secular college established; today – about 30,000 students.
Italy	Bologna	11th century	Juridical studies; first students – mature men from church or state departments
United States	Harvard	1636	Started under church sponsorship; has educated six US presidents, including John. F. Kennedy

4   A NE'ER DO WELL DOES WELL

Is school worth it?

Part 1

INTERVIEWER: Colin, I understand you started from pretty humble beginnings and now you're obviously a very wealthy man. Can you tell us something about your, your early years?

COLIN BARRINGTON: Well I started off – I was in a big family. I was the youngest of eight kids. When I was pretty young my father left us and so we had a difficult childhood I s'pose. There was never really quite enough to eat, if you wanted to have (a) second helping of food you had to eat pretty quickly so that you got in while there was still some left. But it makes you pretty independent when you're in a family that size and you learn the value of things, because things don't come easy, you have to – you have to fight for what you can have and that's helped in later life, definitely.

INTERVIEWER: And what about the importance of school in your …?

COLIN BARRINGTON: D'ah school, I mean I think school's a complete waste of time. You have to go there, I didn't like it there, the teachers I didn't think were any good, you learn about things that are no use to you like history and algebra and, you know, I couldn't wait to leave, to be honest.

INTERVIEWER: So the teachers didn't make it interesting at all?

COLIN BARRINGTON: I s'pose they tried their best, they made it – they seemed to concentrate on people that did well in the exams but to me it was no use so … I didn't learn anything till after I left school.

INTERVIEWER: So when did you leave school?

COLIN BARRINGTON: Early as I could, would have left at the age of twelve, if I could've done but I think was about sixteen, can't exactly remember but as soon as I was able to I left.

INTERVIEWER: And did you have any qualifications when you left?

COLIN BARRINGTON: No. No, no qualifications.

Part 2

INTERVIEWER: And what did you start working at when you left school?

COLIN BARRINGTON: Well, while I was at school I did a little bit of working, you know, in the holidays and at the weekends and I … we used to go down, us blokes from school used to go down to the market – there was a little market not far along the road from school – we used to go down there and very often there was the chance to earn a few bob, because you could relieve the stall holder while he went for lunch and tea and that sort of thing, and in fact I used to work quite a lot then. On one particular stall, we got to know the bloke who ran it well, and I ended up working for him more or less full time after I left school; he didn't particularly wanna (want to)work very hard so I used to run the stall most the time, and that got me into the market work .

INTERVIEWER: What sort of things were you selling?

COLIN BARRINGTON: Well in those days you'd sell anything you thought you could sell, but our stall used to concentrate really mostly on things the other stalls didn't, so we didn't sell clothing and we didn't sell food but often it was sort of gadgets, either things for the house or records – secondhand records – parts for cars, tools, a mixture of things which these days – I suppose the closest thing would be electronics, which of course is what I've gone into since then.

INTERVIEWER: So Colin, how do you then make the break from being a sort of market trader to becoming the big multi-national company that you are now? How did that start?

COLIN BARRINGTON: Well it's like all these things, I think that you know, you have to have a bit of luck; and what happened to me was a bit of bad luck initially. The bloke who owned the stall unfortunately within a couple of years of me leaving school he died … and well, I didn't know what was going to happen then, but his wife who I got to know, she wanted to keep the stall on. I don't know really why because she didn't really need the income, but we had an agreement – we made an agreement that I'd run the stall for

her and instead of me getting paid a wage, we shared the profits –
we split the profits 50:50, and I found that gave me more of an
incentive to make the right deals and do better ...and the stall did
pretty well and after a while I was able to put enough money by to
buy her out ... and the next bit of luck was that I was around about
the time where there was an increase in the electronics industry, a
lot of new developments were happening, particularly out in the
Far East with stereo systems and that sort of electrical goods ... and
I managed to get enough money to combine a little holiday with a
working trip to go and have a look at some of the places where
these things were made and I stumbled on, it was completely by
luck, a company that was in some financial difficulty and I was
able to buy that company out in the Far East and own it. And really
it went from there, and then you just do more selling and you're
looking for new product ranges and it gets bigger and bigger ... and
in those days it was easy to make – well – a reasonable amount of
money, and if you just invest that carefully in the right ventures, it
just grows.

Part 3
INTERVIEWER: Do you feel that you've ... made it in the business
community, do you think that you're accepted by the rest of the
business community, or are you regarded as a bit of an outsider?
COLIN BARRINGTON: Well I feel I've made it, but I feel I'm not
accepted and I never will be accepted 'cause I haven't got the right
accent. I haven't got letters after me (my) name, and I didn't go to
Oxford and Cambridge and these city blokes, they all pretty much
stick together and ... in the end they ... I get the feeling they hope
that people like me fail 'cause we are not the right class for them
really ... and I say, well, I couldn't care less what they think, but
no, you don't fit in unless you've had the right sort of background,
which is why I've done what I've done with my kids. I put their
names down to go to Eton and maybe they'll go to Cambridge
University and all that and even though it's a complete waste of
time – the educational side – I can afford to send them there, so
they will be able to have the snob value when they inherit the business, then they'll be in with the city hoity-toity people, but not for
educational reasons.
INTERVIEWER: But then, Colin, surely, if you've put your children
down for Eton, you must think that education has got some value?
COLIN BARRINGTON: Well I don't think it has, but it will give them (an)

advantage, the kids will have an advantage of having gone to these places and they'll be able to be seen on equal terms with these city people as part of their class.

INTERVIEWER: So then, what would you say then is the secret of success? Is it part education, part luck, part hard work or what?

COLIN BARRINGTON: Well it's three things, I think you gotta (you've got to) be intelligent, you gotta be clever, you haven't gotta have educational qualifications but you've gotta be clever. You also gotta be very lucky and you gotta finally work hard and you gotta have all three of those not just two.

INTERVIEWER: But education comes nowhere in there?

COLIN BARRINGTON: No.

INTERVIEWER: Not at all?

COLIN BARRINGTON: No.

Comprehension answers:

1. Early years: One of eight children; made him tough, independent; learnt value of things
2. Attitude to school: Waste of time; learnt about useless things; couldn't wait to leave
3. Attitude to teachers: They weren't interesting; did their best, but more interested in academic high-flyers
4. When and how he left school: As early as he could, about 16; left with no qualifications
5. Early work experience: Holidays/weekends when at school; market experience, relieving stall-holders, then full time
6. What he sold: Anything – gadgets, records, tools – a mixture
7. How he started his first business: Stall-holder died; went 50:50 with widow; bought her out
8. His big break: Bought Far East company; new product ranges; invested well
9. How his success was received: He thinks he has made it, but not accepted by business community – wrong accent, etc.
10. Plan for children; reasons: Eton and Cambridge – any advantage helps. They must be equal to the city types
11. Secret for success: Intelligence, luck, hard work; not education

Key 6 — A Question of Sport

1 SPORTY TYPES

Word power

1. (i) 2. (j) 3. (f) 4. (a) 5.(g) 6.(h) 7. (e) 8. (c) 9. (b) 10. (d)

talent: talented, untalented, talentless
competence: competent, incompetent
training: highly-trained, untrained, trainer
build: well-built, heavily-built, lightly-built
fitness: fit, unfit, fit as a fiddle etc.

2 SPORT FOR ALL?

Prejudices in sport

Interview 1

HELEN: The problem with sports is there's no place for the less good. You know what I mean? It starts at school where all the attention is paid to the few children who get into the school team – (but) what about the rest of them? They're deemed to be a failure as far as sports are concerned at a young age – so what happens? They lose confidence and get a sort of inferiority complex. This lack of confidence will follow them through the rest of their lives. So every time they think about getting involved, you know joining a squash club, taking some tennis lessons, they shy away through fear of failing. I think it's a real shame. Of course some people are more talented than others in sports, but this doesn't mean they get any more out of it. In fact the reality of a lot of sports clubs is that there's an enormous range of ability – from the almost semi-professional levels of the first team down to a not-so-serious side down at the bottom of the leagues. So there is room for everybody. The problem is a lot of people won't take that risk. I blame society – it's become too competitive – winning-oriented. Sport isn't just about winning.

Interview 2

INTERVIEWER: Julie. You're responsible for promoting sport for women in this area. Are attitudes changing towards sport?

JULIE: Unfortunately not very much.

INTERVIEWER: Why do you say 'unfortunately'?

JULIE: Because I think they should have changed a lot more. Sport is still really a male preserve. Most of the organized sport here is still directed towards men. You only have to look at the playing fields at weekends – all the ball games are being played by men.

INTERVIEWER: Why is that?

JULIE: I feel it's because girls at school are not encouraged in the same way as the boys. But also the boys are much more motivated.

INTERVIEWER: Well, if they're more motivated, perhaps they deserve more opportunities?

JULIE: No. No, no – the reason they're more motivated is because most of the sports role models are men. I mean how many famous female sports stars can you name? OK – tennis stars perhaps, but what about team games like hockey and netball?

Interview 3

HAMISH: Oh, up here, golf is a very democratic sport. Anybody can play. It doesn't cost very much. But look at how it's developed elsewhere. You can't join a club without putting down a small fortune. Developing countries are building golf courses left, right and centre to attract foreign tourists, but none of the locals can afford to join. You don't even need to look so far away. South of the border, many of the golf clubs are the bastions of rich businessmen. I heard about one the other day where you had to put down £2,500 to join. Now who's got that sort of money? Like all sports, golf should be for everybody, in my opinion. Not an elite pursuit for those with more money than sense.

Interview 4

INTERVIEWER: Apartheid in sport was the most visible symbol of the prejudices which dominated South Africa. How have things changed recently?

MARK: They've changed a lot. But you've got to understand it's not just a question of throwing out the old apartheid laws which prevented blacks from playing with whites. Success in sport is all about opportunity. The opportunity to start playing when you're young, the time to practise, the facilities to be available. There's a lot still to be done, but you can see some changes. Blacks are playing more cricket, there are one or two black players in the regional rugby teams.

INTERVIEWER: Surely one or two black rugby players is not much to be proud about? What about providing those opportunities you talked about?

MARK: Well, that's a long-term process. It's not just a question of changing attitudes, it's also improving the standard of living of most black people. You're hardly going to become a top-class sportsman if you're unemployed and living in a shanty town.

Interviewees	What are they unhappy about?	What examples do they give?
Helen	competence	joining a squash club, taking tennis lessons
Julie	male dominance	weekend ball games
Hamish	money	£2,500 to join a golf club
Mark	racial inequality	one or two black rugby players in regional teams

Word power

Extract 1: to shy away; to have a fear of failure
Extract 2: a male preserve; role models
Extract 3: a small fortune; left, right and centre; bastions
Extract 4: a visible symbol

1. I can't afford it. It costs a small fortune.
2. If you shy away from this opportunity, you'll never get a job.
3. She was shocked to find what a male preserve some sports clubs are.
4. Golf courses are appearing left, right and centre.

A question of style

Model answer:

What leads to success in sport? At least 50 per cent is due to your state of mind. Physical fitness, technique and strength all have their part to play but the difference between winning and losing is often down to confidence. Why do you think we see such a growth in sports psychology as a new discipline? Top football clubs wheel in their own sports psychologist before an important game, top golfers retreat for a course of confidence-building after a run of defeats, and even amateur coaches put more and more emphasis on the psychology of winning. Confidence is one side of the coin, but what's the other? Fear is on the other side, and you can see some teams try to instil fear in the hearts of their opponents.

Sound advice

1. (b) You've got to be joking. (a threat)
2. (a) You're her sister, I suppose. (a pleasure)
3. (a) You've been here for a long time? (a question)
4. (a) It is Tuesday, isn't it? (a hope)
5. (b) You'll come to the match, won't you. (an assumption)

3   PLEASURE AND PAIN

Fitness: A matter of opinion

Comprehension answers:
1. Early withdrawal from the circuit and crippling pain.
2. Intensive activity can strain the body and its organs.
3. More relaxed activity leads to less strain.

Getting it right

1. Starting a business is difficult in this economic climate.
2. Thinking of a good example is not so easy.
3. Calling off the wedding now is a bit late.

1. The boxer postponed fighting his next bout until the summer
2. You look exhausted. I would suggest resting for an hour.
3. He persuaded me to take up badminton. I love it now.
4. We need to practise throwing the ball as far as possible.
5. I remember winning my first race at this track.
6. Do you expect to retire from the sport soon?
7. We managed to watch the race on TV.
8. I'd like to try windsurfing next time we're on holiday.

4   GOING FOR GOLD

For love or money?

Part 1

INTERVIEWER: Christal can you tell us something about your main sporting activity?

CHRISTAL SHEFFIELD: Well currently my main sporting activity is powerlifting.

INTERVIEWER: Powerlifting, what exactly is that?

CHRISTAL SHEFFIELD: Well, it's basically – you're lifting weights but you're lifting massive amounts of weights, like for instance a squat, which is basically a barbell across your back and you squat down to your knee and your thigh level and you come back up, that's a full squat, but the average person squats, or should be able to squat, twice their body weight.

INTERVIEWER: That's actually sort of squatting down and then lifting it above your head?

CHRISTAL SHEFFIELD: It's squatting down and lifting back up.

INTERVIEWER: Right.

CHRISTAL SHEFFIELD: Right, so powerlifting is lifting massive amounts of weight, past what you would do just for regular toning exercises.

INTERVIEWER: And how do you train for that then?

CHRISTAL SHEFFIELD: Right now I run and I do stretches, I do aerobics, and then … you pick your weights, and you set your limits and you increase your weight each time you train, and try and see how many reps you can do.

INTERVIEWER: What's a rep?

CHRISTAL SHEFFIELD: A repetition is what it is. A repetition – and if you pick a weight that you can do comfortably, then you go up in weight and you do that continuously and that builds your strength.

INTERVIEWER: Right, right, and what's exciting for you in this sport, what do you get out of it?

CHRISTAL SHEFFIELD: Self-satisfaction basically, I – growing up I was a tomboy – and I always knew I would not be one of the little small, dainty girls and I was, I was an athlete and I just – I was always told I was strong. So this is just something I got into on a whim, say – well let me see if I can do it. And I did it and I kept doin' it and I've won three competitions so far and I'll just keep doin' it until my body just says that's enough, it's time to stop.

Part 2

INTERVIEWER: So you obviously spend an awful lot of time on your sport, a lot of hours per week, I mean are you paid in any way for your participation in it?

CHRISTAL SHEFFIELD: No, unfortunately I'm on a very, very amateur level; that's why I say it's done for pure enjoyment.

INTERVIEWER: Right. I mean do you think that's right, do you think you ought to be paid for it?

CHRISTAL SHEFFIELD: Well, no, not yet. I'm not to the best that I know I could be in order to be paid, so until I get to that level I'm comfortable with the self-satisfaction in the trophies and medals I get.

INTERVIEWER: Right, but there is a professional side to your sport?

CHRISTAL SHEFFIELD: There is a professional side and I'm nowhere close to that amount of weight yet.

INTERVIEWER: Right, but when, when you get to that stage or for the people who are already in that stage, what are the rewards like for them, what are the financial rewards?

CHRISTAL SHEFFIELD: One competition I remember reading on … one … the first place was like $35,000, that's just for one competition.

INTERVIEWER: Yes, so it's an extremely well-paid sport.

CHRISTAL SHEFFIELD: It's extremely well-paid but it's a lot of training.

INTERVIEWER: Yeah, do you think that's right that, that the people should be paid that much?

CHRISTAL SHEFFIELD: If I was at that level yes, yes but there are some sports who shouldn't be paid for.

INTERVIEWER: But what about things like athletics, the Olympics and so on? What do you feel about that? Should people be paid for participating in sports like that or not?

CHRISTAL SHEFFIELD: So-so, I have mixed feelings on that. I'm happy with being a good athlete. I'm happy with the recognition. Some people do it for advertising chances, promotions and for the money, but some people – it's a mixed thing there …

INTERVIEWER: I mean a lot of people do give up a lot of their time don't they, to do it.

CHRISTAL SHEFFIELD: … They do give up a lot of their time and some of this, these are people's jobs, this is what they do on a daily basis – is train.

INTERVIEWER: Yes.

Part 3

INTERVIEWER: Well obviously there are many sports where there are quite a lot of expenses that you have to incur in order to practise that sport.

CHRISTAL SHEFFIELD: It's true.

INTERVIEWER: In your case in terms of weights and so on. Do you think there should be any way in which the money generated by the professional sport should be ploughed back in … into helping amateur athletes improve?

CHRISTAL SHEFFIELD: I think there should be, but if you look at it from their standpoint they'll look at it – 'well I wasn't given the help so why should I turn around and help someone else?' – and that's really not the way to think. Some people start with meagre weights, things in the back yard, things of that nature and I think each of these athletes that are getting paid this astronomical amount of money should put it back into the communities they came from, to build up the gyms and make it a free membership for these people to go train with the proper weights and the proper kind of training, or even give it to Special Olympics for the kids who really need it.

Comprehension answers:
1. No, it's lifting massive amounts of weight – more than just regular toning exercises..
2. No, she has a barbell across her back. She bends into a squat and then straightens up again.
3. No, she was a tomboy, she was never dainty, but she always knew she was strong.
4. No, she's at an amateur level and she does it for pure enjoyment.
5. No, she thinks in her sport they should be paid, but not in all sports.
6. No, some people do it just for the recognition; others do it for advertising, promotions and for the money.
7. No, some of them think that, but she thinks they should put it back into the communities they came from, etc.

1 ROADS TO SUCCESS

Is it who you know?

Extract 1

There are no easy breaks in life. I've always said you make your own luck. I started right at the bottom of the pile as a fitter and made my way to the top. At times it was hard, but Australia is a culture in which hard work is respected.

Extract 2

Successful business is all about good communication. International business is even more about good communication. Of course you have to make the right contacts, but after that it's a question of knowing what to say and how to say it. Speaking the customer's language is much the most important factor in securing the deal.

Extract 3

The world's changed a lot since I worked my way up the ladder. I think who you knew was very important in those days. I think it's become much more competitive – it's still a matter of contacts but that's not enough – you've got to be a real go-getter – someone who'll really push for what they want.

Extract 4

In France, it's still important which school you went to – there's a sort of unofficial club. Just look at the background of all the chief executives of large companies in France – they all have a very similar educational background. But you know, it's not a bad thing in my opinion – it gives the country a fairly coherent industrial strategy.

Answers:
1. hard work 2. communication and language 3. drive/dynamism
4. education

Getting it right

A: What did you think of his chances?

B: Pretty good. He's got an extremely impressive c.v.

A: Well you'll be interested to know he didn't do very well in the interview. In fact he performed absolutely terribly.

B: So, who got the job?

A: I don't think they've decided yet. It's between a woman from sales. She's quite a bright spark. You know she's more highly qualified than anybody else in the company. Somebody said she's got a PhD in philosophy.

B: And who's the other candidate?

A: He's an external candidate. Apparently he's a fully-fledged chartered accountant.

B: But I thought we needed a new sales manager.

A: Sure. He's also worked for a fairly long time in marketing overseas.

B: That sounds quite useful.

A: Yes, it does. Anyway, they're going to be making decision next week.

B: The sooner the better!

2   RULES OF THE GAME

Dealing internationally

Part 1

INTERVIEWER: Alex, could you tell us a little bit about your experience in conducting international business?

ALEX MOTT: I've been with Nokia for the last two years and we operate across Europe. Although I am focused in the UK, I do work with our people across Europe – so I'm in Rome, I'm in Helsinki, I'm in Dusseldorf probably every quarter. Previous to this position I was working as an international consultant and I worked in Prague and in Moscow. So I work in marketing right now with advertising, and then while I was in Eastern Europe I was working more on the ground with the people teaching them sales skills, marketing skills and what market economies are all about.

INTERVIEWER: So with all that experience, how much more difficult would you say it is to organize deals with international partners as opposed to dealing with – inside one familiar country?

ALEX MOTT: I think the biggest hurdle that certainly an American would have is this cultural … and the cultural understanding, because you can't offend people you can't be too pushy – Americans are typically very, very pushy . But I think what you need to do is understand the culture and to get, get into the – the area that you're gonna (going to) be operating in and live – live the life there if you will, not spend all your time at four-star hotels saying, 'well I've now spent time in Prague and I understand it.' It's spending time with people, going to local restaurants so that you've got a much better understanding on a cultural level.

Part 2

INTERVIEWER: And, what sort of preparation do you do before you go to a country? Do you study the customs of the country, before you go?

ALEX MOTT: Yeah, you certainly want to read books at the least. One of the biggest advantages anyone could ever have going into a different culture is to learn the language. I would say that without a doubt that'll be your biggest plus if you do do that. But, it is more difficult because it takes more time, because you're a foreign person, and so there is this period of time where you've gotta (got to) adjust to them as oppose to them adjusting to you which they're never gonna do.

INTERVIEWER: And in some of these countries you've been working in … I mean were there things that amused you or shocked you when you first, when you first set foot on their soil?

ALEX MOTT: Well one of the, one of the funniest stories actually that wasn't, wasn't when I first got into Moscow but – I was doing sales training and so we were going out on calls and at this point in time we hadn't given any of the sales representatives any cars to travel round Moscow so they used to hitchhike across Moscow, and so here I am – a quote unquote western businessman – hitchhiking with one of our female sales reps and we walk out of the front door of the office building and she sticks out her finger to pick up a ride and an ambulance pulls over. And so there weren't any seats in there except for the front one – and I didn't talk Russian at that point in time so she sat up front and I was in the back with the gurney and we went across Moscow – it was really something that doesn't happen in New York, let's say.

INTERVIEWER: In the back with the what, with the gurney?

ALEX MOTT: With the gurney, yes, with the –

INTERVIEWER: The stretcher?

ALEX MOTT: – Yeah, the stretcher.

Part 3

INTERVIEWER: Alex, what sort of factors do you have to take into account when you're trying to put together a complex international deal?

ALEX MOTT: Some of the key factors are the future plans, not only of your company or your business but also of the people that you're dealing with and that's very, very difficult, depending on what kind of economy you're looking into. For instance when we were going into … what was Czechoslovakia, when we first went in there in 1991, we elected to set up two different companies, one based in Prague and one in Bratislava. We had the foresight to look into the fact the country was gonna split into two republics as it is today, and that was very, very effective in keeping both businesses going up till the present day. So planning, being able to look forward and plan for something like I just said –

INTERVIEWER: It's a political analysis really?

ALEX MOTT: – Yeah, in one sense for that country it certainly was, you've obviously gotta have a very long-term commitment and so instead of just being there and making money quickly, we had to plan for the future.

INTERVIEWER: When you're dealing with foreign customers, I mean are there any sort of special customs or conventions that you personally have had to take into account?

ALEX MOTT: Well I think some of the, the key ones are gesticulations. I now am living in and working in the UK and the various signs that you might have for victory, etc. are quite dramatically different than the ones that we have in the US. So you certainly want to be aware of what you're saying with your hands, because some people are very expressive with them, and it can upset an awful lot of people very very quickly.

INTERVIEWER: Do you find that people in the UK react badly if you sort of over-gesticulate?

ALEX MOTT: Yeah, they – well I think they see it as very American first of all. But gesticulations, your tone of voice, your – how forward you are with people can either, you know, allow them to accept you very quickly or put them off and ruin deals for you.

INTERVIEWER: So would you say there are any particular dos and don'ts when you're doing business internationally?

ALEX MOTT: OK, well – one other 'do' that I would say that was very effective for me is, in some of – in the Eastern European countries that I was working in – one effective thing was I would get down and do the copying or I would make a cup of tea for people, and what that did for the locals was show a commitment, that I wasn't there just to stay in the posh hotel and tell them what to do and what not to do, but I was rolling up my sleeves and demonstrating that I was there to help their business; and that certainly will take you a long way into getting a deal or, again, showing the commitment that you're behind the joint venture that you might be working in.

Comprehension answers:
1. I am focused in the UK.
2. While I was in Eastern Europe I was working more on the ground.
3. You can't afford to offend people, you can't be too pushy.
4. Read books; learn the language.
5. He had to hitchhike with a female sales rep. They got a lift across Moscow in an ambulance, and he had to sit/lie in the back with a gurney (stretcher).
6. The idea of himself as a sophisticated US business executive having to travel in such an unusual vehicle.
7. False. It was a good idea to do this in Czechoslovakia, because the country split into two.
8. False. It can also be misunderstood and give the wrong impression (ruin deals).
9. False. He used to do the photo-copying for people and make the tea, so they didn't regard him as a posh outsider.

Word power

1. We can put you up until Thursday.
2. He's always putting her down.
3. I'm just putting you through.
4. It's important to put some money by for emergencies.
5. It's putting me off.
6. He's put in for promotion.

3   STAR APPROVAL

Dangerous liaisons

Comprehension answers:
1. Pepsi withdrew sponsorship because of accusations of drug addiction and child molestation.
2. Nobody remembers the brand.
3. (a) clean, but not boring (b) street credibility (c) connection between product and celebrity

Word power

1. (d) danger   2. (h) for example   3. (g) support   4. (a) vouch for
5. (b) worthy of support   6. (c) departure   7. (f) beyond reproach
8. (e) match

Completed sentences:

1. He is a credible candidate for the presidency, partly because of his squeaky clean private life.
2. The sudden withdrawal of the leading candidate from the election illustrates the pitfalls of modern-day politics.
3. He had hoped for support from many quarters. In fact he only persuaded one minister to sponsor his candidacy for the leadership.

4   A QUESTION OF HONOUR?

Big business and the moral maze

Comprehension answers:

1. Adoption of written codes of conduct.
2. Over-lavish Christmas gifts and entertainment.
3. Poaching former colleagues.
4. Because state control is sufficiently tough.

Word power

1. (c) unethical   2. (b) ruthless   3. (b) unselfish 4. (c) practical 5. (c) lenient 6. (b) tough 7. (a) moral 8. (b) selfish

Completed sentences:

1. He argued that you couldn't afford to take ethical/moral considerations into account. Business was far too tough at the moment for such niceties.
2. He was accused of being corrupt, of having bribed government officials.
3. This was not a moral decision, it was purely pragmatic; we had to decide whether to invest now or later.
4. The company was accused of being very lax with its own rules and regulations. It appears that some unethical employees had been selling their shares shortly before recent profit announcements.

Getting it right

1. He was too easy-going.
2. She was not strict enough.
3. He was not ruthless enough.
4. She was too altruistic.
5. They were too easy-going.

Key 8 Health

An ideal service?

Speaker 1
What I'd like to see is more emphasis on primary care – you know, better local family doctors, health prevention initiatives. I can't help but feel that too much money is poured into hi-tech medicine – you know, pin-hole surgery, magnetic scanners. All this sort of investment benefits the few and advances the frontiers of medicine, but what about some low-tech medicine – the sort of medicine which encourages us all to look after ourselves better – that's where the emphasis should be, in my view.

Speaker 2
Of course enormous advances have been made over the last few years – infant mortality is down, the mortality rate as a whole is much better. But the differences between the rich countries and the developing world are still enormous. In my country, Ghana, we've made great strides in curing some of the communicable diseases such as TB and diarrhea, but we simply cannot support the level of health care found generally in the developed world. Most of the problems are to do with a lack of money – we need money to educate and to treat our people better.

Speaker 3
What we're creating in this country – Britain I mean – is a two-tier system where the rich have access to swish private hospitals, instant referral to specialists and the best the medical profession can offer, while the rest of the nation is increasingly offered a second-class national health system, where budgets are being cut, hospitals are run by finance-driven accountants and success is measured purely in the number of patients that one GP or hospital can turn over in a day.

Speaker 4
Sure, we are going to have to make cuts. The problem is that our patients' expectations far exceed the available resources. Over the last twenty years we have all been living longer and better lives – well, that's great – but there's a cost and it's one which the country is finding it difficult to cover. We're going to have to make difficult choices – keeping an old people's home open or investing in a new cancer research centre, buying a new scanner or carrying out an immunization scheme. There aren't going to be any easy answers.

Speaker 5
The problem is that we have all an obsession with health. We worry about what we eat, how much we exercise, and all the little aches and pains. We can't accept that our bodies get tired and start to run down – we think we can stay young and very strong into our seventies – well maybe we should try to do that, but I can't help feeling that there are more important problems like giving good health care to countries in the Third World.

Country	Patient/doctor	Area of concern
Canada	Patient	*too much hi-tech medicine, not enough low-tech primary care*
Ghana	Doctor	differences between rich countries and the developing world
Britain	Patient	two-tier health system (public and private)
Australia	Doctor	excessive health demands leading to difficult choices
Italy	Patient	obsession with own health vs basic health care for Third World

1. We can't pour endless money into health.
2. All the time we are advancing the frontiers of medicine.
3. We have made great strides in tackling diseases.
4. The problem is expectations exceed resources.
5. Governments have to cover the costs.
6. There are no easy answers.
7. We all worry about our little aches and pains.

Word power

Model answer:
People write letters about the most extraordinary problems.
A Mrs Swan wrote complaining of a problem she had recently *faced* with her neighbour – Mrs Kenton. This had started out as a seemingly *trivial* problem of noise. She found that she was often woken at night by low-level vibration emanating from her

neighbour's house.

She decided to *tackle* the problem directly by speaking to her neighbour. Together they walked round the house trying to *identify* what was *causing* the problem. Following many unsuccessful attempts to *spot* the source of the problem, they decided to swap houses for one night.

The next morning, Mrs Swan emerged from her neighbour's house without having slept a wink. Mrs Kenton, on the other hand, had slept like a new-born baby. The two ladies had a much more *serious* problem to *tackle* now. It appeared that Mrs Kenton's snoring had been the source of the noise all along.

2   ROBODOC?

Medicine 2010

Comprehension answers:
1. The elderly.
2. Yes - the robots will put their human counterparts to shame.
3. Life enhancement and eugenics.

Getting it right

Other combinations are possible:
1. Robotic surgery is bound to be introduced sooner or later.
2. Medical information such as medical records may be sent down the line using a modem.
3. It's quite likely that some single-gene diseases will be curable by the end of the century.
4. Multi-gene diseases such as heart disease can't possibly be cured for some time.
5. A cancer cure is unlikely to be found before the end of the century.
6. It's improbable that a cure for AIDS will be found for some years.
7. Scientists could identify the gene responsible for multiple sclerosis in the near future.
8. We should be able to use telemedicine to reduce health costs soon.

3   HEALTH HAZARDS

Tobacco: Cash crop or killer?

Comprehension answers:
1. The writer suggests that smoking is closely connected with a nation's sense of liberty.

2. There are several reasons: dependence on tobacco as a cash crop; century old traditions; association with ' the good life'.

Word power

Demographic changes underlie many of the problems national health care systems will face in the 21st century. In the developed world the number of older people has been on the *increase* for many years. This change in the demographic structure has been caused by a marked *decline* in the birth rate. As the population *grows* older, the rate of disease *rises*. In addition, the demands for more sophisticated health care has *rocketed* over the last 20 years. While it is true that the rate of contagious diseases has *plateaued*, the rate of serious congenital conditions such as heart disease have *grown*. Of course, one of the 'problems ' is diagnostic tools have improved greatly, often leaving us in no doubt what we are suffering from. Perhaps the only way to control *spiralling* health costs is reduce expecatations. However, for the moment there is no sign that health care costs are *flattening* out, let alone *decreasing*.

4   FRINGE BENEFITS?

An alternative view

Part 1

INTERVIEWER: Lily can you tell us a little about your background and training in alternative medicine? How did you come to it?

LILY KYAN: Yes, I was trained in Taiwan – in Taiwan National University and it's a western medical college. So although it's a Chinese university it's a western medical college.

INTERVIEWER: I see.

LILY KYAN: They teach western medicine there and I have a BSc degree in rehabilitation medicine, which means a branch of western medicine in that particular college.

INTERVIEWER: I see.

LILY KYAN: And from there on I was trained in acupuncture as post-graduate training and the same in this country. A lot of people who are now having acupuncture training, they are taking up post-grad-uate training and we have colleges here set up for students, like for doctors or nurses, physiotherapists, dentists for example, they can all join this particular course.

INTERVIEWER: After they've done their more traditional training.

LILY KYAN: Correct, yes.

INTERVIEWER: Oh I see. And what are the main fields that you're working in now? Is it purely acupuncture or are there other fields?

LILY KYAN: I am working in acupuncture as well as Chinese herbal medicine. I am a member of the British Acupuncture Association and also a member of the Chinese Acupuncture Association in Taiwan and a member of registered Chinese herbal medicine in this country.

INTERVIEWER: Is that in any way connected to aromatherapy – is that the same thing?

LILY KYAN: Not at all, not at all. Aromatherapy is again another branch of alternative medicine, but a very, very small branch. Any acupuncturist, if they're interested in aromatherapy, can of course learn aromatherapy quite easily and use it in their practice – when and if necessary.

INTERVIEWER: But what is Chinese herbal medicine exactly?

LILY KYAN: Chinese herbal medicine is a part of Chinese medicine – as acupuncture. Acupuncture and Chinese herbal medicine together and massage therapy all form part of Chinese medicine so they use herbs of mostly plant origin, root, leaves, twigs, anything of the plant or the flowers for that matter. Sometime (they) also use animal origin items.

INTERVIEWER: Like what?

LILY KYAN: Like tiger bone for example, which is not very welcome in this country but we don't use them in our own practice now. But I very rarely use animal origin items. There are also minerals one can use, it's also part of Chinese medicine, but I mostly use plants. But having said that, there are a few animal origin items that we have to use in our practice because they are very effective. A small example – beetle shells – that's a shell of a beetle after the beetle has matured and crawled out of it. It's valuable to treat a skin condition.

INTERVIEWER: Really, in what way, what do you do with it?

LILY KYAN: (If the) skin itches, you brew them together with the rest of the herbs to help to stop the itchiness.

Part 2

INTERVIEWER: What, what sort of patients come to you, what sort of people go to alternative medical practitioners?

LILY KYAN: All sorts really. I mean most of them, having tried the conventional medicine – western medicine – and never (having) had any result, apart from that they possibly ended up suffering from side effects.

INTERVIEWER: From drugs?

LILY KYAN: From drugs of course, and they may be taking four or five different drugs already, and the symptom(s) they are producing are such a combination of symptoms it's almost (too) difficult to differentiate what is causing what any more. But most of them are also suffering from a great deal of pain when they come and the symptom has not been reduced whatsoever by taking medicine – by taking western medicine.

INTERVIEWER: Yeah, are there any particular ailments that people come to you for?

LILY KYAN: Many, many ailments – skin condition(s) for example, irritable bowl syndrome for example, gynaecological symptom(s) for example, I mean female problems, gynae problems we have, we've got so much – so many of them… That kind of case, when we treat them with acupuncture they respond very well.

INTERVIEWER: And in some cases it actually cures the symptom, doesn't it? I mean, it's a lot more than just a painkilling treatment.

LILY KYAN: It's a lot more than that, it's not just curing the symptom, it's also going further than curing a symptom. It actually has a physiological change in the body.

INTERVIEWER: And is this cure – this change – is it permanent?

LILY KYAN: Permanent is something that I tend to avoid using in my practice because it's very individualized. You have to assess the patient carefully and what other problems they may be suffering from.

INTERVIEWER: So there's a degree of psychology as well as physical cure?

LILY KYAN: Yes, that as well, yes, and emotional, too.

Part 3

INTERVIEWER: Lily, do you think it's possible that alternative medicine will acquire the same status as traditional medicine in the West?

LILY KYAN: This is very difficult to say, one day we hope that it would be, but … it will take a few more years before its (it) actually get(s) to a similar status as conventional medicine. Obviously in China it is equivalent to western medicine and it works side by side with western medicine.

INTERVIEWER: Really.

LILY KYAN: Yes, in a hos–, the same hospital, then, they have western medicine and acupuncture and traditional Chinese medicine all working together, but in the West I would say it will take a few more years, but we are now gradually accepted.

INTERVIEWER: Before, I mean, it was thought to be a bit on the edge?

LILY KYAN: Hocus pocus – yes indeed. A lot of doctors still feel that it needs scientific proof, but really it's been proven enough. If only they opened their eyes to look at it.

INTERVIEWER: Yes, 'cause it's not just – I mean for people that don't know this – it's not just sticking needles into somebody's body where you feel like it, I mean it's an extremely exact and complicated science.

LILY KYAN: That's right. That's quite right. It's a very complicated science. And in fact, I feel that you cannot just use molecular explanation(s) you know, scientific explanation(s), it's just too much in it, because there (is) a lot more spiritual stuff as well involved in acupuncture, but we won't go into that!

Comprehension answers:

1. She trained in Taiwan (western medical college), then completed post-graduate training in acupuncture.
2. Acupuncture and Chinese herbal medicine.
3. A very small branch of alternative medicine.
4. Plants: roots, leaves, flowers, etc. Animal origin items: tiger bone, beetle shells. Minerals.
5. All sorts. People who have tried western medicine and had no result – except possible side-effects from drugs.
6. Skin conditions; irritable bowel syndrome; gynaecological/female problems.
7. Not yet, but gradually improving (although in China they have western and Chinese medicines working side by side in the same hospitals).
8. She wishes they would open their eyes (to the benefits of Chinese medical techniques).

Key 9 The Media ■ ■ ■ ■

1 WHAT SCANDAL?

Creating a scandal

Extract 1

I can't understand why they make such a fuss. I mean, who cares whether some second-rate politician is having an affair with an opera singer or an office cleaner? The problem is the papers are convinced this is what we all want to read about. Personally I find it all pretty sordid.

Extract 2

I think they deserve all they get. After all, we elected them and so we have every right to expect a certain standard of behaviour from them ... they're always going on about standards of morality. Well, I say they shouldn't be where they are if they don't know how to behave. No, I reckon we have every right to be informed of what they're getting up to and they all seem to be getting up to something.

Extract 3

Well, as far as I can see, it's all about selling newspapers. I don't think they could give a damn about what public figures get up to really, but a bit of muckraking sells more newspapers. I'm sure none of the journalists or editors live like angels.

Extract 4

I don't mind them hounding politicians and the like to an early grave, or more likely resignation – they chose public life and so they have to live in the public eye. No, what I can't stand is the way the tabloids pick on the private individual. Just the other day, there was a story about a young mother who had had to give up her two children – it was splashed all over the paper, taking a moralizing tone as usual.

Extract 5

It's strange what your newspapers choose to call a scandal. In France, the fact that a politician has had a child by another woman would never make the front page – in fact we have laws to protect the privacy of this sort of information. In my opinion, the British are obsessed with this sort of voyeuristic journalism.

Extract 6

The trouble is we'd like to judge people on their achievements, but it's human nature to judge them on their failings. It doesn't matter how much a man or a woman has achieved in public life – what great works they've done – no, they can be undone by one indiscretion – being over helpful to a friend in need can easily be interpreted as corruption, being seen with a partner other than your spouse can always be portrayed in a disreputable light, even minimizing your tax liabilities – an objective we all share – can backfire, if you're in the limelight. The media knows how we work and they exploit it.

Attitudes expressed:

1. Only the papers care about scandals. The speaker finds it sordid.
2. We've every right to be informed.
3. Scandals are used to sell newspapers.
4. It's OK to publicize scandals about public figures, but not private individuals.
5. The British are obsessed with sex scandals.
6. It is human nature to judge people on their failings.

A question of style

1. Personally, I find it disgraceful. (s)
2. Don't you think we should ban all such reports? (m)
3. I reckon we need to consider all the options. (m)
4. Maybe we could consider inviting the editors for a meeting?(w)
5. I'm sure there's another way of approaching this problem. (s)
6. As far as I can see, the media does more good than bad. (m)
7. I wonder whether we shouldn't discuss this further? (w)
8. I don't give a damn what you think about this. (s)

Strong: disgraceful, appalling, dreadful, scandalous
Moderate: poor, disappointing, dull, tedious, mediocre
Weak: acceptable, adequate, satisfactory

2   LANGUAGE LIMITS

Expletives deleted

Comprehension answers:
1. (i) sex and genitalia (the forbidden) (ii) scatological (filth)
   (iii) blasphemous (sacred)
2. Restricted film.
3. The tabloids avoid the use of swear words whereas the quality
   press uses them when justified.

Word power

1 (d) expletive 2. (g) filthy 3. (f) profane 4. (h) serious papers 5.
(c) popular 6. (j) blacklist 7. (a) judge 8. (i) prurience 9. (b)
nervous 10. (e) justify

1. The serious/quality press are nervous/skittish about running
   sensational scandal stories as they do not want to be accused of
   prurience/lasciviousness.
2. The film last night did not warrant/justify the use of swear
   words/expletives. I found it very offensive.
3. The censors obviously deemed/judged the programme to be
   blasphemous/profane. But surprisingly the church said they felt
   the expletives/swear words were very mild.

3   FORM AND SUBSTANCE

Image maker

Part 1

INTERVIEWER: Meryl – as a communications consultant, part of your
work is concerned with preparing politicians, or would-be politicians for appearances in the media. Can you tell us a little bit about
how you set about preparing them for those appearances?
MERYL GRIFFITHS: Yes I can. It's quite difficult with politicians because
of course they think they're very powerful people, and very
powerful people quite often don't like being told about their weaknesses and areas that they need to develop. So first of all I have to
get to know them quite well, analyze what's maybe preventing
them coming across in the way that they want to come across.
Once we've decided what that is, then it's a question of in a sense
re-educating old habits. I mean the way that we behave is all about
habit, we behave in a certain way because that's the way we
always have done. They then need to become consciously aware of

what they're doing, which can be quite a painful process. Once they become aware they have to bring in the new habit and keep working at it until it replaces the old habit.

INTERVIEWER: Do you think every politician needs media training or are there, is there such a thing as a natural communicator on TV?

MERYL GRIFFITHS: I'll take those two separately 'cause I think they're quite – two distinct questions really. I do think all politicians need some kind of media training. I think that the pressures on them, it's quite exceptional pressure in a way, representing the country, whatever ... I think that their job is too important for them to risk getting it wrong. The second question was whether there is such a thing as a natural on television. I don't think there's necessarily such a thing as a natural on television. I do think there are people who are more natural at communicating generally, and I think that's important to draw that distinction – yes, television is quite exceptional in its demands because it really does focus very tightly on what they're doing and can exaggerate behaviour through the medium, but someone who's a natural at communicating I think, gets that balance between achieving their objective and getting across what they want to get across, and establishing some sort of ... relationship if you like, or connection with the people that they're talking to. If it goes too far one way or the other, for example if someone is too concerned with objective they may come across as though they're haranguing or lecturing the people they're talking to. If they go too far the other way, then they may well be too conscious of the reaction of the people that they're talking to, too concerned with their approbation and approval and may try and dilute the message, or whatever.

Part 2

INTERVIEWER: So what are the most common faults of someone who is not a natural then?

MERYL GRIFFITHS: One point that's really important is that nobody ever invents new behaviour, so if there is a fault they won't suddenly invent a new behaviour for television. They won't start doing something they don't do in everyday life.

INTERVIEWER: Right.

MERYL GRIFFITHS: Right. So for example, if their fault in general communication is to talk too quickly or maybe to talk too loud or to mumble, then under pressure in the television studio they're likely to do it even more so. I only ever knew one man who did something under pressure that I don't think he would have done in everyday life. He wasn't a politician, he worked in the stock exchange. He stood up in front of an audience of three hundred people and he clutched his bottom for the whole half hour. I don't think he would have walked through the stock exchange clutching on to his vulnerable bits.

INTERVIEWER: So can you give us some concrete examples of those small faults which can be magnified under pressure?

MERYL GRIFFITHS: Yes. There's an example of a former British leading politician when he was speaking live to large audiences he was fine – he came across as very passionate and very committed to what he was saying. One of his tendencies was to speak in long sentences – when he was carried away with the passion of it all. On television it came across as though he was … had a slightly woolly intellect, it seemed as though he might have lost sense of what he'd said at the beginning of the sentence, and certainly some of the viewers listening may well have lost sense of it as well. With a fault like that we needed to work very much on shorter sentences, putting in full stops, putting in clean pauses so that he got those gear changes, he got those changes of thought and he also had some structure in the logic and the argument of what he was saying.

INTERVIEWER: Right …

MERYL GRIFFITHS: Let me give you another example on delivery and how it can influence the message. Another person I was working with recently – whenever they spoke they sounded tentative and as though they were seeking approval, and the reason why was that at the end of every sentence they pitched up at the end of the sentence in the way that I'm trying to demonstrate now. And can you hear it sounds as though I'm seeking some sort of response from you every time I speak?

INTERVIEWER: Yes, you want me to say 'that's right' every time.

MERYL GRIFFITHS: That's right. With that person what I had to do, and it was difficult this one, was to encourage them to pull the pitch down at the end of a sentence. Now can you hear when I'm talking to you now that it sounds as though what I'm saying is much more cut and dried. The moon really is made of cream cheese. I dare you to argue with me, John.

INTERVIEWER: I believe you, I believe you!

Part 3

INTERVIEWER: Do you advise people on what they wear, how they do their hair, this sort of thing?

MERYL GRIFFITHS: Yes I do sometimes, I – I think it's only part of the visual impact. Other aspects are probably more important, things like facial expression are more important; you know that's the most important visual aid. But clearly clothes are going to make a difference and a lot of it is about common sense really. The politician needs to decide is he appealing to the electorate as they are, or is he appealing to them in some sort of aspirational sense i.e.– i.e. looking as though they … say you've got a politician whose going in and working with people who are not very wealthy, don't have a lot of money to spend on clothes, and he comes in in some hugely expensive suit, they may resent that, so he may want to dress more in the way that they dress. But on the other hand he may want to appeal if he's saying to that electorate, 'Yes I can get you out of this situation, I can help you become wealthier,' you know if that's what he decides they want. Then, maybe dressing in a way that they could aspire to dress is important as well, but I think it's less important than some of these other things.

INTERVIEWER: So Meryl, moving on to the effects of all this, do you think that the power of the media is beginning to hide or in some way disguise the force of political messages? Putting it another way, do … can you wrap up an unacceptable message by the tricks of your trade so that the public find it acceptable?

MERYL GRIFFITHS: Yes, I do think there's a danger that we're beginning to oversimplify the message. The difficulty is I'm not sure we can do – what we can do about it. There's been a lot of research done on how audiences make the judgements that they make. This is to do with first impressions and it's to do with attitude as opposed to understanding the message. The king of the researchers is a chap called Albert Marabian who works in the University of California, Professor of Psychology there. He reckons that when we're making judgements about people in terms of their credibility or whatever, we judge it 55 per cent on the visual, that's facial expression, the things I've been talking about – it's eye contact, it's movement, it's body language, clothes, visual aids; 38 per cent on the sound of the voice, volume, use of pitch, use of pause, the pace, the tone of voice, which leaves 7 per cent on the words. Now that's the way we make the judgements we do. So for example, if a politician needs to get across a really difficult message and his behaviour is in any way hostile or defensive or aggressive, then that's going to taint the message. If he's getting across the message and the words are assertive in the same way, but his behaviour is considerate and respectful and seems to be indicating some sort of wish for involvement and empathy with the people he's talking to, then that message is gonna (going to) be much more acceptable – because he's saying that this is what I need to do, this is my objective, you may not like it, but I also understand how you feel, in behavioural terms. Does that make sense?

INTERVIEWER: Yes it does, but I mean do you think we ought to be worried about that? Can we be deflected by this sort of manipulation into areas that we would really be much better not getting into?

MERYL GRIFFITHS: Yes, I think we should be concerned. I think we shouldn't be complacent about these issues, I don't think it's all the politicians' fault; they are delivering what often the journalists want, you know they want to wrap it up in sound bites and just give a quick potted version of what's happening around the world very quickly, so they are fitting in with that. But as a member of the public I do think we need to check other sources the whole time, we need to look for more in-depth interviews rather than the news readers' sound bite. We need to check political comment and check things from different angles the whole time, because I think as members of the public it's very easy for us to look for reinforcement of our original ideas – you know, we've made up our minds on something and what we're looking for is reinforcement. We don't want those views necessarily to be challenged. Now that's our fault because we're lazy.

Comprehension answers:

1. No, she has to re-educate old habits.
2. No, she says there are people who are more natural at communicating generally, not just on TV.
3. No, they exaggerate their existing faults – except for her one example!
4. No, it came across as if he was woolly. He was passionate. She had to shorten his sentences, give his speeches structure, etc.
5. No, sometimes that may cause resentment, but he could also appeal to their aspirations/hopes by wearing an expensive suit – as if he is saying that this is the sort of thing/wealth he can bring to them.
6. No. The percentages were:
   55% visual factors (facial expression, eye contact, body language, etc.)
   38% sound of voice (volume, pitch, pace, tone)
   7% the words themselves (the meaning)

7. No, if the words are strong, then he has to have a considerate, respectful and empathetic delivery in order to be respected.
8. No, it's not always the politicians' fault. They deliver what the journalists want (i.e. sound bites, etc.).
    The public should check things from different sources.
    Too often people just want reinforcement of their often existing opinions and ideas – this is what she calls lazy.

4   A CHANGED WORLD?

Communacopia

Comprehension answers:
1. Rupert Murdoch's 'News Corporation'.
2. Because of the media domination of such people as Rupert Murdoch.
3. Superhighways: communication cables which can carry limitless information. Communacopia: a world where the technologies of entertainment, information, transaction and telecommunications have combined.
4. Existing mainstream media (TV and newspapers); individualized information/programme sources.

Getting it right

Model answer: *Note that other linking words are possible.*
I get up and turn on the box for the breakfast news. *Consequently* I can't hear my newspaper being pushed through the letterbox. As I struggle bleary-eyed downstairs, I can hear the broadcaster solemnly announce an increase in the number of unemployed. *Nevertheless,* I determine to remain optimistic in my search for a job.
However, there are very few grounds for optimism as I've been looking for a job for more than a year now. As I munch my way through a bowl of cornflakes, I start to skim through the job advertisements – *of course* there's practically nothing that would suit me. *However,* I note down the telephone number of a job hotline which I've not seen before. When I phone them later that morning, I get through to an answerphone telling me to fax them my curriculum vitae *as well as* a letter indicating my job preferences *especially* salary range. The message ends by requesting a registration fee of $50. Not surprisingly I decide against pursuing this line of enquiry with an answering service.

1 HERE IS THE NEWS

Hurricane! A radio report

STUDIO NEWSCASTER: Reports have been coming in throughout the day of the terrible devastation caused by Hurricane Herbert. Our first report comes from Brian Robinson who is in the Bunesh capital, Newindi. Brian, how do things look?

BRIAN ROBINSON: Hurricane Herbert hit the coast at 4 o'clock local time this morning. It is now 11 o'clock at night and the scene is one of utter devastation. The first area to be stricken was the coastal strip. Satellite pictures enabled us to watch events as they were unfolding – a massive 10 metre wall of water carrying everything in its wake. The hurricane then continued its toll, moving inland towards the capital. It has now blown itself out a little, but you can probably still hear its devastating force outside the hotel.

It is too early to say what the death toll will be, but officials here are reckoning at least half a million victims will have been drowned under the first impact of the wall of water. In Newindi itself many buildings have been destroyed by the winds. Emergency services expect to be working round the clock trying to locate and save the many people trapped in their houses. However, the strong winds at present are preventing many people from going out on the streets to help in the rescue effort. The President appeared on television this evening and declared a state of emergency. In a two-minute talk he asked the international community for help with what he called a natural and man-made disaster. This is Brian Robinson for SatNews from Newindi.

STUDIO NEWSCASTER: Thank you, Brian. And we will be bringing you more from Newindi as reports come in. As we heard, the President called the disaster natural and man-made. President Nasur has long been an arch critic of the West, claiming that the West's wilful neglect of the environment has been doing irreparable damage throughout the globe. I am now joined in the studio by Paul Cunningham, the leader of Eco2000. So, was today's hurricane a man-made catastrophe just waiting to happen?

PAUL CUNNINGHAM: Of course it was. Since the end of the 20th century we have been seeing a whole series of extreme weather events – droughts, floods and violent storms, of which Hurricane Herbert is just one. You see, there are three links in the causal chain. First, our treatment of the environment, second the global change which this causes, and third the climatic changes caused by changing the face of the earth.

STUDIO NEWSCASTER: Can you explain those links in a little more detail?

PAUL CUNNINGHAM: Certainly. In simple terms, if we continue to deforest our earth, overgraze our land and pollute the air and water, then our planet will be incapable of sustaining us and it will die. The violent climatic changes that we see today are the terminal throes that our planet is in.

STUDIO NEWSCASTER: Yes but –

PAUL CUNNINGHAM: Inactivity now undoubtedly means more extreme weather events, causing death and destruction on an enormous scale. And as the climatic changes reach ever further from the equator and from the poles, then no area on this planet will escape. It is only by a radical reappraisal of our lifestyles that we have any chance to save the planet. The Earth Summit scheduled for next year in Rome must urgently address the issues of protecting the earth's air, soil, water, and living organisms.

The reporter
Name of hurricane: Hurricane Herbert
First area affected: coastal strip
Height of wave: 10 metres
Estimated casualties: half a million
Type of disaster: natural and man-made

The environmentalist
Three types of extreme weather events: droughts, floods and violent storms
Three examples of environmental damage: deforestation, overgrazing and pollution of air and water
Four issues for Earth Summit: protecting the earth's air, soil, water, and living organisms

---

Getting it right

1. The summit will enable world leaders to discuss environmental issues.
2. The terms of the conference prevent/stop the leaders from taking decisions on global environmental actions.
3. As we have seen, the leaders have been incapable of reaching/haven't been able to reach a consensus.
4. On another occasion, the industrial lobby would have been capable of influencing/could have influenced the decisions.

5. The level of concern will stop/prevent them from avoiding the issues.
6. Yesterday, protesters were prohibited/prevented/stopped from entering the conference area by the police.

Word power

1. discuss   2. tell   3. said   4. speak   5. talked

1. I suggest that we discuss the points in the following order.
2. I'm afraid I cannot disclose that information because it is confidential.
3. I hereby declare the meeting closed.
4. After many hours of discussion they finally accepted our proposals.
5. Let me emphasize once again how important I consider this point to be.
6. I would like to add another point to the agenda, namely the benefits brought by modern science.
7. I feel that I must reply to the criticisms made by the previous speakers.
8. The protesters allege that industry has destroyed the environment.

2   BEING AWARE

Getting started

Icons (left to right from top row): nuclear energy; acid rain; recycling; global warming; fire hazard; litter; no smoking; diminishing forests; forest fire; oil/chemical pollution; water pollution

Word power

advertisement: ad or advert	fanatic: fan
examination: exam	high fidelity: hi-fi
photograph: photo	telephone: phone
aeroplane *(BrE)*: plane	bicycle: bike
gasoline *(AmE)*: gas	television: TV
omnibus: bus	motion picture *(AmE)*: movie
condominium *(AmE)*: condo	personal computer: PC

3   THE RIGHT OF REPLY

Sermons or survival?

Comprehension answers:
1. Politicians and industrialists

2. Food, water and air
3. No other species can both adapt the environment and adapt to its changes.

A question of style

Part 1

1. We are concerned about all the algae in the pond. I know you have agreed to do something about it. So, do you think you could clean up the contaminated water before the summer?
2. We're very worried about the effect of air pollution on children. We have noticed an increase in respiratory problems, so could you tell me when you will have reduced the gas emissions?
3. You do realize that although coal is a renewable resource, it takes an extremely long time to renew it. By the way, do you happen to know how much coal we have left?
4. We recently formed a small group to monitor food distribution to a number of countries. We'd like you to act as a member of this group.

1. (A)   2. (I)   3. (I)   4. (A)

Part 2

1. Do you think you could tell me where exactly you plan to put the containers for waste paper, glass, cans and plastics?
2. European regulations for air pollution have been strengthened. Do you know what the currently permitted air pollution levels are?
3. I wonder if you could tell us how long the dangers from radioactivity and nuclear waste will last?
4. Do you think you could present the results of the survey into the usage of public transportation?
5. Please don't be under any illusion about the effect of the destruction of the world's rainforests.
6. In many countries CFC aerosols have been banned. I wonder if you could take the first step in this country by stopping the production of CFC aerosols?
7. Our trees are still affected by acid rain. Do you think you could put pressure on our neighbours to reduce their emissions of toxic chemicals into the atmosphere?
8. Our waters are a national disgrace. I'd like you to reassure us that steps are being taken to clean up our rivers and seas so that they meet the agreed standards.

Direct	Neutral	Indirect
2 5 8	1 4 7	3 6

Word power

Something which:	Negatives:
– can be repaired: reparable	irreparable
– can be done: possible	impossible
– is fit to eat: edible	inedible
– changes often: changeable/variable	unchangeable/invariable
– can be easily broken: breakable	unbreakable
– gives enjoyment: enjoyable	unenjoyable
– is worth a lot of money: valuable	invaluable *(opposite in form, but not in meaning)*
– is preferred: preferable	–
– can be divided: divisible	indivisible

---

4   A HEALTHY BALANCE

To add or not to add?

Part 1

INTERVIEWER: Jean-Luc, these days, we hear a lot about the chemicals that are added to food. What type of chemicals are these, exactly?

JEAN-LUC DUBOIS: Er … before answering that question, I'd just like to say that 'chemicals' is maybe not the appropriate term. You see, we are all made of chemicals in the first place – I would prefer it if we could speak about additives. That is really a more appropriate term to use in the food industry. OK? So what type of additives do we put in food products? Well, in the food industry we use preservatives for instance, anti-oxidants, emulsifiers, stabilizers, colourings and also flavourings and sweeteners. For baking we use anti-cracking and raising agents, like er, for instance, baking powder.

INTERVIEWER: I see. Well, that's quite a long list there Jean-Luc, what exactly is the purpose of these things you have mentioned?

JEAN-LUC DUBOIS: The purpose is to improve quality, and what we mean by quality is having a better product, for instance a product which has a longer shelf life. Or we could, by using additives, improve the texture, or increase the variety of a product range. Or, we could have a product which is safer in terms of micro-organisms.

Part 2

INTERVIEWER: OK. You said that – that one of the effects is that these additives make the product safer, but are there any ill-effects on the human body?

JEAN-LUC DUBOIS: Oh, no, no. As far as I know, no, no. I don't see any reason why any of those additives we use could be dangerous, unless of course you have an allergy.

INTERVIEWER: An allergy?

JEAN-LUC DUBOIS: Some people have an allergy to even peanut protein, and they may die from a drop of perfectly organic peanut oil ... so it's really quite difficult to answer that question. But apart from an allergy, there is no risk, the additives are more or less safe.

INTERVIEWER: So, Jean-Luc, you said that one of the reasons for using additives is that it makes products safe, or safer. Does this mean then that there are no side-effects, no side-effects at all with the use of additives on the human body?

JEAN-LUC DUBOIS: Well, as I told you, well I don't know of any additive which could be dangerous for humans. The first thing is that the quantity – the quantity of the additive, by definition, is very small, and an additive which might be considered dangerous, like SO2 or vinegar acid, is used in such small quantities that it is no real problem for the human body.

INTERVIEWER: Yes, but we do read in the newspapers about the risks caused by additives ...

JEAN-LUC DUBOIS: Yes, but we do not use any harmful elements such as – mercur?

INTERVIEWER: Mercury.

JEAN-LUC DUBOIS: Mercury – or lead. All the additives we use are destroyed by the body, so I don't see any reason why there should be any problems, either for our own bodies or for other parts of the food chain.

INTERVIEWER: So what you're saying is that there are no direct risks. But what about the indirect risks transmitted through the food chain from animal feeds and things like that?

JEAN-LUC DUBOIS: Well that's not really my field. All I can say is that we don't use any products that might affect the food chain.

INTERVIEWER: Now there are a lot of environmentalists who are campaigning very strongly against the use of chemicals in food products. Why do you think they are so outspoken and vociferous against the use of chemicals?

JEAN-LUC DUBOIS: Yes, of course – well, that's a very difficult question. How can I put it? Campaigns start usually from ... one thing, one particular point of view, and this can sometimes get, shall we say, distorted out of all proportion. I don't see why anyone should campaign against additives in food. I think sometimes it's political. I don't see it as a campaigning issue. It's up to the consumer to decide whether he wants to have less choice and avoid all additives, or if he wants the variety and convenience of modern food products.

Part 3

INTERVIEWER: So, if you look into the future Jean-Luc, do you think the use of additives will increase or decrease?

JEAN-LUC DUBOIS: Yes, I think that the use of chemicals – as most people think of them – will go down. As our knowledge of food science increases we will see a rather more – how shall I put it – sophisticated approach, like using for instance natural anti-oxidants such as rosemary extract, and using fewer synthetic compounds and acids, more 'enzymes?' …

INTERVIEWER: Enzymes.

JEAN-LUC DUBOIS: Enzymes, which will affect micro-organisms directly … I think that overall, we will probably be using less in terms of quantity, and we'll focus more on specific types of additive.

INTERVIEWER: Jean-Luc, thank you very much.

JEAN-LUC DUBOIS: Thank you.

Comprehension answers:
1. He prefers the term additives because we are all made of chemicals.
2. Anti-oxidants, emulsifiers, stabilizers, colourings, flavourings, sweeteners, anti-cracking and raising agents (like baking powder).
3. The main purpose is to improve quality.
4. The quantities are very small; there are no harmful elements used; they are all destroyed by the human body.
5. He says they often have one particular point which gets distorted out of proportion. Their motives can be political.
6. (Refer to the recording script for details.)

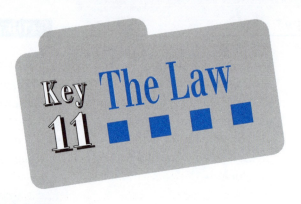

Key 11 The Law

1   ORIGINS OF LAW

Word power

science and art of government: politics
study of the production and distribution of wealth: economics
abstract science of space, number and quantity: mathematics
set of morals and moral principles: ethics
science of sound: acoustics
practice of and competition in physical exercises: athletics
science of language: linguistics

Noun	Adjective
drama	dramatic
theory	theoretical
hero	heroic
practice	practical
system	systematic
critic	critical
magic	magic(al)
science	scientific
grammar	grammatical
sympathy	sympathetic

2   PRACTICES OF LAW

How fair is the jury system?

Comprehension answers:
1. By vetting the jury before they took up their jury service.
2. Because they didn't want to find their neighbour guilty of committing the crime of theft.
3. Because a defendant can now be found guilty on a 10-2 majority verdict.

Getting it right

1. A jury is a group of laymen who decide factual issues in criminal and civil trials.
2. (Al)though the jury was used in non-anglo-american countries, it lost power and became far less common in the 19th and early 20th centuries.
3. Jury trials occur most frequently in the United States where 90 per cent of all jury trials in the world are held.
4. As/Because some individuals may be biased, they are excluded from jury service.
5. In Europe, unless a two-thirds majority agree that a defendant is guilty, he must be acquitted.
6. In criminal cases, the jury's duty is to decide questions of fact, while in civil trials they decide matters of liability and levels of damages.

Word power

Legal procedures	People involved with the law
trial	accused
case	judge
evidence	jury
verdict	defendant
	witness
	juror
	foreman

1. A person is put on trial for an offence that he or she is alleged to have committed.
2. The person who stands trial for a criminal offence is called the accused/defendant.
3. In a criminal trial witnesses may be called to give evidence.
4. In a civil case the person against whom the complaint is made is called the defendant.
5. A jury is usually composed of 12 men and women from the community and one of them acts as the foreman.
6. Some professionals, such as policemen and lawyers, are exempt from serving as jurors.
7. After the evidence has been heard, the jury retires to decide upon the verdict.
8. Finally, in criminal trials, the judge passes sentence.

Getting it right

Punctuation model:

Avoid writers, because they invariably construct their own case, based upon dramatic values, and ignore the law and the facts; professors and those who live cloistered lives generally, because they are too easily shocked by the raw facts of life; former policemen and private watchmen, because the chances are that at one time or another they have been outwitted by criminals.

3   LEGAL SYSTEMS

Getting started

Note: there may be some variation from country to country with regard to matters such as trespass.

palimony (family law/civil law)   bigamy (family law/criminal law)
breach of contract (civil law)   unfair dismissal (commercial law)
trespass (civil law)   negligence (civil law)
theft (criminal law)   murder (criminal law)

Constitutions and procedures

Extract 1

PRESENTER: First, we hear from an American lawyer.

AMERICAN LAWYER: In the United States, every body from a social club right up to Congress must have a constitution: a set of rules and doctrines and practices that govern the way that body operates. And having a constitution is the mark of a modern state, spelling out the rules that need to be followed. It gives rights and freedoms to individuals so that they know what the limits of their behaviour are; in other words it provides protection. Now having a written constitution confers a number of additional major benefits. Two major points I would consider important: firstly it means that the citizen can find out the extent of his rights, duties, freedoms and obligations by referring to the relevant document; and secondly American lawyers can similarly consult these documents to advise their clients on their rights and freedoms. A written constitution, it simply provides certainty.

Extract 2

PRESENTER: Next, an English law professor gives his view.

ENGLISH LAW PROFESSOR: Of course, what the Americans love to do is to point to their written constitution and hold it up as the mark of a highly developed system of government. Just because we don't have a written constitution, just because it isn't there in black and white, doesn't mean that the British citizen enjoys any less protection under the law. In fact, I'm bound to say that it is just the opposite; the very absence of a constitution makes law-making more flexible, more responsive to an ever-changing world. The ordinary law of the land, as it's practised throughout the land, is the essence of the British constitution. And of course, this body of law cannot be found in a single document. But then again, no document today could possibly contain all the minutiae needed to govern a complex society such as ours.

Extract 3

PRESENTER: How does the law operate in France?

FRENCH LAWYER: Here in France, we and our European Union partners follow what is called the Roman or continental law system, whereas in England the system is called the common law. What differentiates the two systems is more a question of origins and procedures rather than substance. I mean, under both systems, there is the rule of law. However, the Roman system is derived from the formal written codes – such as the ones the Romans had. The Romans, you see, during the expansion of their empire, tried to keep all of their territories under a unified system of law. Of course, they were administered locally by the magistrates. But the state was considered a powerful force – elevated above individuals and their rights.

Extract 4

PRESENTER: Gisela, you're a practising lawyer in Germany. What's your view on these different approaches to the law?

GERMAN LAWYER: Well, under the inquisitorial system, such as we have in Germany, the judge plays a much more active role. He is there to find out the truth and he will guide the proceedings in that direction. Not only does he do this during the trial, but also before. He supervises the police and can order a police investigation. In fact, it is the judge who decides whether to prosecute or not. He is an inquisitor, charged with finding out the truth. And that is what court proceedings should be about. Not a competition, as in the adversarial system, such as they have in England, where they let the best man win. Justice is not about the skills of the lawyer and how well he or she can put your case. It's about justice for the individual.

Extract 5
PRESENTER: A British lawyer compares the results of the procedures.
BRITISH LAWYER: Under the adversarial system, the question facing the court is: Is there sufficient evidence to convict someone? Has the prosecution proved their case beyond reasonable doubt? If not, the accused is acquitted. Under the inquisitorial system, the court is trying to find out the truth. Of course, that takes much longer. And having done that, an appropriate verdict is reached. Now the result is that there are far more convictions under the inquisitorial system, a much higher conviction rate. But I'm not convinced that those extra convictions are, in fact, people who are guilty. No, I am sure it is better that guilty people are acquitted, as under our system, than that innocent people are convicted.

Completed notes: Extract 1
Subject discussed : written constitution
Three advantages: spells out rules to be followed; citizen can find out rights, duties, etc.; lawyers can consult documents

Extract 2
Subject discussed: British constitution
Main advantage: law-making more flexible

Extract 3
Subject discussed: continental law system
Purpose: unified system of laws

Extract 4
Subject discussed: court procedures
Under inquisitorial system: judge is there to find out the truth
Under adversarial system: competition lets the best man win

Extract 5
Subject discussed: inquisitorial versus adversarial systems
Result: more convictions under inquisitorial system
Speaker's view: better that guilty are acquitted (as under adversarial system) than innocent convicted (inquisitorial system)

A question of style

1. What both parties can do is interrogate the witnesses.
2. It is the citizen who benefits from not having a written constitution.
3. It is in the legal procedures that we can see differences.

4. What each side tries to do is prove their case.
5. Not only does the adversarial system ensure a fairer trial, but it also provides a quicker one.
6. What the law should give is justice for all. It is justice for all that the law should give.

4   CRIMINAL MASTERCLASS

White collar crime

Part 1

INTERVIEWER: Mike, you're a computer consultant and you've advised many companies on their computer installations – and we understand that – that one of the fastest growing areas of white collar crime is actually in computer-aided crime. Why should that be?

MIKE FEILDING: This is basically a result of the spread of computers into all areas of business at the moment, and whereas communications always used to be done with pieces of paper and chitties and things, nowadays everybody uses a computer to communicate all sorts of information throughout the entire company. So instead of putting a forged signature on a cheque nowadays, you would put the equivalent authority illegally into the computer and hopefully release money for yourself at the far end.

INTERVIEWER: Well, can you give us some examples of the type of frauds that people try and get away with?

MIKE FEILDING: I think the classic ones that hit the headlines are always the big ones where somebody, probably working inside a bank or some other financial institution, manages to redirect an outgoing movement of preferably thousands of pounds into their personal bank account. Whereupon a colleague half way round the world manages to swiftly withdraw it and disappear, and the banking people are actually left weeping and wailing. Figures published quite recently have said that for all the furore that the banks make about bad debts and home loans and outstanding personal debts and everything else that's costing them so much money, in fact they are now losing far and away in excess of that through internal fraud from people who are actually removing monies from the bank.

INTERVIEWER: Employees of the bank?

MIKE FEILDING: Employees of the bank in, in conjunction with people outside the bank.

INTERVIEWER: Right, is it normally then brought about by people who are insiders, or can outsiders sort of hack in to various companies and steal – steal funds from outside, or is that much more difficult?

MIKE FEILDING: No, it's normally done by insiders – the hackers that you read about normally are doing it for the fun of gaining entry and then to prove they've done it they cause some mayhem. Just as any old white collar crime always used to be, to make it effective you have one guy on the inside and one guy on the outside and the fact is that you don't do it with a forged slip any more, you do it by telling the computer to authorize the slip.

Part 2

INTERVIEWER: So Mike, given that white collar crime generally is, is crime done at a desk and not somebody coming up with a shotgun and threatening physical violence, how easy is it to detect and to prevent it?

MIKE FEILDING: I think this depends on the extent to which you have used the computer to assist you with the crime, and also exactly what the particular crime is. The simplest use of the computer that comes to mind – or computer system – was the gentleman who took his paying-in book into the bank – now a paying-in book of course is pre-coded with your account number and details – and he tore out the slips and put them in the tray where people normally come when they haven't their paying in book and want one. So the next 25 or whatever people who paid in wrote their own name on the slip and the amounts of money. This went through to the computer, which of course completely ignores the handwriting, took the number, paid it all into his account. Now that was fairly easily monitored because it was the bankings for a particular day and as soon as the first one was discovered they could see quickly whose account it went to – not too big a problem tracing it. If you're performing a fraud on an international bank which is moving millions of transactions internationally, and you are putting one rogue transaction into that and all you're doing is changing the address that the transaction's going to – to your own bank account rather than your supplier's bank account – then it becomes very difficult to actually locate it because the figures all add up to the correct amount, it's just one of them flew off in the wrong direction.

INTERVIEWER: What about the punishments that are meted out, I mean first of all to the man who put his own paying-in slips in, and then to the international financiers who are shuffling funds around. What are the range of punishments that people get?

MIKE FEILDING: The ranges I think are quite various. They were certainly very various early in the situation, because the courts basically had no precedent on how they should organize this. The story of the man with the paying-in slips supposedly ends with the judge fining him one dollar, and he insisted that the banks bear the cost of the transactions because since they'd been careless enough to take all these pre-printed slips, they really were to blame. It seems to me justice was done there. On the international scale there are so many 'ifs' and 'buts' that a straight fraudulent transaction – if you can prove who actually altered the code – will get a fairly stiff penalty nowadays. The difficult crimes assisted by computers I think are on the international financial market, such as we have seen and will no doubt continue to see for many years, where shares are artificially raised and lowered through computer buying and selling or computer assisted buying and selling, and it is very difficult then to prove that there was a basic crime such as an insider dealing crime or any malevolent intent.

Part 3

INTERVIEWER: So given the difficulty in proving this sort of crime, then what sort of measures can be taken to try and prevent it?

MIKE FEILDING: This is very much like preventing any form of crime in your business. I feel that largely it starts off by keeping a well-motivated staff working for you so that they're not moved to actually thieve from you in the first place. Having done that, the normal principles which used to be applied to people in different departments such that people only knew about the stuff in their department and not in a next department meant that security was carefully applied by those who had a 'need to know'. Nowadays this 'need to know' is applied within computer systems by identifying people by passwords normally, and attaching various rights to these passwords. These passwords must be kept – obviously – safe, they should be changed regularly, just in case there's been accidental transmission of them. Staff have to be aware of the importance of their password. This I find one of the most difficult things to get across to staff because if somebody can't log in through their own password, somebody will say, 'Oh well, use mine.' And this of course means that they are delegating authority where they do not actually have the right within the company to delegate that authority.

INTERVIEWER: Isn't that part of the whole sort of concept whereby people don't regard this – this area of crime as being terribly serious, it's somehow on the margins of crime, not to be compared with violent crime?

MIKE FEILDING: I think this is very true. Unless you're actually starting star wars by hacking in to the main military centres it is very difficult to cause physical pain or physical fright to people through computers, and I don't think that the general public perception of crime through a computer has anything that attaches to personal affront. It's very much such an individual thing done so far away with the numbers that we don't understand and the general public don't understand the technology involved anyway.

INTERVIEWER: So what sort of chance have we got of eradicating this sort of crime?

MIKE FEILDING: Well I think we have to remember that if somebody really wants to pick the lock on your door they will do so. If they need to pick the lock on the computer and they're trying hard enough they could probably do so. But if you take a practical, common-sense approach to keeping the security of your computer systems as secure as you would your paper systems, then you will normally have no trouble at all.

Comprehension answers:

1. Reasons for spread of computer crime: All sorts of people using computers now, throughout companies.
2. Example of computer frauds: Big ones – transferring thousands of pounds to account in other countries.
3. Insiders or outsiders to blame? Normally have to have insiders. Outsiders hack in for fun. Usual set-up one guy outside, one on the inside.
4. How easy to detect or prevent? Depends on extent and type of fraud.
5. What sort of punishments? Quite varied. Courts had no precedents.
6. Measures suggested to protect security: Keep staff well-motivated; give passwords on need-to-know basis; keep passwords safe and change regularly; ensure staff realize their importance.
7. Why public doesn't take this crime more seriously: Difficult to cause physical pain or fright through computers; it's usually a thing done far away, with numbers we don't understand and technology we don't understand either.
8. What chance of eradicating white collar crime? If someone really wants to get in, they will, but practical common-sense measures usually ensure no problem.

1 WHAT'S ON TV?

 Pleasing the people? A panel discussion

PRESENTER: Peter Nixon, you've been making programmes for TV for many years. How do you see your role?

PETER NIXON: Well, as far as I'm concerned, TV is a medium of entertainment and my job is to entertain people. So, you have to ask yourself what entertains people. Basically people like to be engaged – you need to spark some emotion – it may be fear, sympathy, anger, amusement – but you've got to get a reaction. Audiences nowadays are very demanding. They're looking for very high-quality programmes and if they don't get them, they switch off.

PRESENTER: You mentioned the emotions. What about programmes engaging their intellectual curiosity?

PETER NIXON: I suppose you mean documentaries. Yeah, well … to be frank, you've only got to look at the ratings to see what the viewer thinks of the worthy documentary. No, our job is to entertain, not educate.

PRESENTER: Susan Brackton, I don't think you would agree?

SUSAN BRACKTON: I certainly wouldn't. I think it's arrogant of Peter to talk for all viewers. Many have been switching off their TV sets for good over the last few years, simply because they can't stand a lot of the mindless entertainment that's broadcast into their homes. No, I think a balance is needed. Of course there's a place for high-quality escapist drama but there is also an important role for the documentary. Many viewers would like to be better informed about the issues which dominate the news or which have a crucial impact on their own lives.

PRESENTER: Jackson Peters, how do you think TV is going to win back some of its viewers?

JACKSON PETERS: Well, I think it's got a hard task. You have to realize what TV is competing with. The range of entertainment choices from spectator sports through to virtual reality games is getting wider by the day. Nevertheless I think TV will remain at the centre of our home-based entertainment at least for the next 20 years or so. If we just take ratings as a measure of what the viewers would like to watch – then we would broadcast 24-hour soap operas. But I'm pretty sure that even if soap operas do attract the largest number of viewers on a regular basis, this doesn't mean they would want to watch their favourite soap all evening. No, there has to be a mix between light entertainment, drama, quiz shows, live sport, and certainly, documentaries. TV producers should never be missionary in their desire to educate their audiences, but they need to respect the average viewer's well-developed critical faculties.

PRESENTER: So you'd go for balance.

JACKSON PETERS: Absolutely.

PRESENTER: Just to finish our discussion, let's find out what your own preferences are. Peter?

PETER NIXON: I'm afraid I'm a real quiz addict, especially sports shows.

PRESENTER: Susan?

SUSAN BRACKTON: The only programme I watch regularly is Question Time – you know the weekly debate with politicians?

PRESENTER: And finally Jackson?

JACKSON PETERS: I must admit I don't like missing *Casualty*, you know, the hospital drama series?

Viewer	Opinions
1. Peter Nixon	TV for entertainment not education, getting emotional reaction is important.
2. Susan Brackton	Balance needed. Documentary responds to demand for information.
3. Jackson Peters	Competition from other entertainment media. Balance important.

Getting it right   1. (g) 2. (b) 3. (h) 4. (d) 5. (a) 6. (e) 7. (f) 8. (c)

Word power   1. soap opera.   2. documentary drama.   3. quiz show / game show.   4. chat show/talk show.   5. period drama.   6. sitcom

From classics to jazz

 Part 1

INTERVIEWER: Meredith can you tell us something of your background in music? Where did it all start?

MEREDITH WHITE: I was brought up in New Zealand and I started playing the piano at the age of seven. It was in the family, my – my mother played the piano and her mother was a teacher of violin and piano, and my grandmother actually was given a scholarship to study music in London, but because they weren't very well off she couldn't afford to take up the scholarship, so she just stayed in New Zealand and taught, and I got the same scholarship – I won the same scholarship many, many years later, and I was fortunately able to take it up, so I came to London and studied at the Royal Academy of Music for three years –

INTERVIEWER: And that was piano?

MEREDITH WHITE: – Studying piano, that's right, classical piano and I'd already done a degree in New Zealand in music so I'd had quite a lot of study really, quite a lot of academic work as well as performance, but concentrating on performance.

INTERVIEWER: What performance, what sort of performances had you given over there?

MEREDITH WHITE: I'd done recitals and a few concertos, Beethoven One, Beethoven Five, piano concertos.

INTERVIEWER: So classical music was very much in your blood?

MEREDITH WHITE: Yes, indeed.

INTERVIEWER: So when did you start becoming interested in jazz music?

MEREDITH WHITE: Well not until very late. I wasn't interested in jazz at all when I was younger and I didn't play any jazz, I didn't even listen to jazz so it was a very sudden change for me. Just –

INTERVIEWER: What happened?

MEREDITH WHITE: Well I decided that it would be an interesting avenue to explore and so I started off by having a few lessons, which is not the usual approach to studying jazz or to learning jazz, so I certainly didn't learn it on the streets. I had some lessons and I started listening to jazz, which is – you know that's the best way to learn – and I wasn't all that keen at first, it took a while. I think it's really an acquired taste if you haven't been brought up with it.

Part 2

INTERVIEWER: So it was just like another branch of your classical studies for a while, is that right?

MEREDITH WHITE: I wouldn't say it was a branch of my classical studies. It was really going off in a different direction. I didn't really know where it was going to take me.

INTERVIEWER: It was just sort of casual interest which grew?

MEREDITH WHITE: Yeah, and after a couple of years of listening and taking it very slowly I decided I'd like to do it more, more intensively, and I was very fortunate to get a place at the Guildhall School of Music which has a one year post-grad jazz course, and so for a year I was just immersed in jazz – and I was able to study it and listen to it and be surrounded by it for a whole year which was wonderful, and I just – I really loved it, I really developed a passion for it.

INTERVIEWER: But how – what are the main differences in the way that people can teach you how to play classical piano or classical music and then how to play jazz? How do you get taught to play jazz?

MEREDITH WHITE: The main thing is the listening, I mean you start from listening , that's just absorbing the genre really, but there are certain techniques – it's a bit like learning a language, in a sense that there's a structure to it. I think often people don't realize, they think it's all improvised and there's a lot of improvisation in jazz obviously, but it's improvising within a structure. So the structure is like the grammar – you need to learn the grammar in the way that you do when you learn a language, and within that there's certain vocabulary that you also need to learn and explore, and once you've grasped those basics, then you can be much freer to express yourself in the same way that you do with language.

INTERVIEWER: Is it a harmonic structure or is it based on keys or progression?

MEREDITH WHITE: It's based first of all on form. So for example, if we take a jazz standard like say, 'Autumn Leaves' that is very well known – that's a 32-bar form and you go round that 32-bar form first of all playing the tune and then you explore the harmony of it by making melodic lines and then you come back to the tune at the end, but it's always within this 32-bar structure.

INTERVIEWER: So could you explain to us some of the differences in the style and the way you play jazz as opposed to classical piano?

MEREDITH WHITE: Well it's partly what you play, but it is more important how you play it, and for me the main difference between classical music and jazz is that jazz has an underlying pulse in a much stronger way than classical music does, because in classical music the pulse can be bent more. The pulse is more flexible, so that in jazz the pulse is agreed by the players but once it's agreed its very, very solid. So jazz musicians talk a lot about feel, the way you feel the music and groove – and that's really, really important. So that's the rhythmic …

INTERVIEWER: Is 'groove' the same as 'feel'?

MEREDITH WHITE: I suppose so, more or less. So I'm really talking about rhythm here – the rhythm is different.

INTERVIEWER: So how would that then compare then, with a classical piece? I mean, take a piece of Beethoven, is there only one way to do a Beethoven sonata?

MEREDITH WHITE: Well there's – within a Beethoven sonata the performer has a certain amount of freedom, but only within the style that's really laid down, so one always tries to do what Beethoven wanted.

Part 3

INTERVIEWER: What about the different types of audiences for classical and jazz? Are there huge differences? Which do you prefer playing to?

MEREDITH WHITE: I prefer jazz audiences. One of the things I really like about jazz is that it attracts people from all walks of life and all ages as well, although I have to say it's quite male-dominated so that can be a problem – it hasn't really been a problem for me, but I think that's changing fortunately, but it's still the case. The way that I relate to an audience when I'm playing jazz is quite different from playing classical music. I feel I have a lot more contact with the audience. Usually the audience is closer so you're not up on a stage with that huge space between you and the audience. The audience is more responsive because they tend to clap after solos and you feel you're getting more reaction as you go along, as you're playing.

INTERVIEWER: Do you think you get more personally out of playing jazz than you do classical music?

MEREDITH WHITE: I do, yeah, very much more. It's opened a door for me, a whole new way of approaching music, which I think is very exciting because I feel I can express myself a lot more in jazz.

INTERVIEWER: What sort of plans have you got for the future, I mean are there some big bands that you've played with or have you got other plans?

MEREDITH WHITE: I play in lots of different bands, but I would like to get my own band together at some stage in the future. I haven't done that as yet. I haven't really needed to 'cause I've had (a) reasonable amount of work with, with various bands – I've played with about eight different bands – and I'd like to do more writing 'cause that's something that I really enjoy – writing music and arranging, and I'd like to do more of that, but that's very time-consuming.

1. Because they weren't very well off, she couldn't take up the scholarship.
2. I decided it would be an interesting avenue to explore.
3. I wasn't all that keen at first … I think it's really an acquired taste.
4. It's a bit like learning a language, in the sense that there's a structure to it.
5. … first of all playing a tune, then you explore the harmony of it.
6. … for me the main difference between classical music and jazz is that jazz has an underlying pulse in a much stronger way than classical music.
7. One of the things I really like about jazz is that it attracts people from all walks of life, and all ages as well.
8. … the audience is more responsive, because they tend to clap after solos and you feel you're getting more reaction as you go along.
9. It's opened a door for me, a whole new way of approaching music, which I think is very exciting.

Sound advice

At the beginning	In the middle	At the end
pneumonia	light	bomb
psychology	half	column
gnat	campaign	
knight		

NB *Other examples are possible.*

3 **FUTURE TRENDS**

Comprehension answers:
1. Escape from home and relief from competitive stress.
2. Communal experience and individual interactively.
3. Dial-up virtual reality techniques.
4. VR booths in city shopping and entertainment areas, home devices, applications for cultural venues such as museums.

Word power

Other combinations are possible:

1. The climbers were attempting a virtually impossible route up the north face of the mountain.
2. The critics all thought the new series was absolutely essential viewing.
3. The match always had a wholly predictable outcome.
4. The new system requires highly skilled technicians to maintain it.
5. They supported their request for money on a fundamentally flawed argument.
6. You should see her incredibly funny impersonations of leading politicians.
7. Don't bother to turn on the TV. There's a singularly unamusing comedy programme on at the moment.
8. It was a tantalizingly close result. They lost in the end by just half a point.

A question of style

1. (g)   2. (h)   3. (b)   4. (a)   5. (c)   6. (d)   7. (i)   8. (f)   9.(e)

ACKNOWLEDGEMENTS

The authors and publishers wish to thank the following for permission to use copyright material:

Financial Times for adapted material from Diane Summers, 'Dangerous Liaisons', *Financial Times* 18 November 1993; from David Buchan et al, 'Laying down a code of honour', *Financial Times,* 26 May 1993; and from 'The power of choice, with the promise of a digital future', *Financial Times,* 6 October 1993;

Fuji Photo Film (UK) Ltd, McDonald's Restaurants Ltd, Mercedes-Benz (United Kingdom) Ltd, Peugeot Talbot Motor Company plc and Virgin Atlantic Airways Ltd for permission to use their company logos;

TMS (UK) Ltd for the source material on pp 28 and 29. The Margerison-McCann Team Management Wheel is a registered trade mark of Prado Systems Ltd. For precise pinpointing of a person's preferred role, it is necessary to complete the Team Management Index, a questionnaire developed by Charles Margerison and Dick McCann, which also provides a detailed personal profile for reference during discussions aimed at improving teamwork.

Oxford University Press for adapted material from Paul Sieghart, *The Lawful Rights of Mankind,* 1985;

Stephen Pile for material from *The Book of Heroic Failures,* Routledge London, 1979;

Random House Inc for material from *Going International* by Lennie Copeland and Lewis Griggs, Random House New York, 1985.

Reed Consumer Books for material from Jilly Cooper, *Class,* Methuen London, 1979; and from Roger Cook and Tim Tate, *What's Wrong with Your Rights?* Methuen London, 1988;

Sports for adapted material on Muhammad Ali from Stewart Hennessey, 'Sporting Hero Column', *Sports,* May/June 1994;

The Economist for adapted material from 'The future of medicine', *The Economist,* 19 March 1994. Copyright © by The Economist, 1994; and for adapted material from Anthony Smith, 'The electronic circus', *The Economist,* 11 September 1993. Copyright © by The Economist, 1993;

The Guardian for material from Madeleine Bunting, 'The overworked society', *The Guardian,* 16 March 1994. Copyright © 1994 by The Guardian.

The authors and publishers wish to acknowledge the following photographic sources:

Allsport: 65/Allsport Historical Collection, 66/Mike Powell, 72;

John Birdsall: 131

The Image Bank: 1/David de Lossy, 5/Infocus International, 13/Grant V. Faint, 17/Janeart Ltd, 24 r, 27 main/Peter Hendrie, 27 inset/Ted Kawalerski, 39/Don Klump, 40/John P. Kelly, 51/Chip Chalfant, 52/Werner Bockelberg, 63, 85/Janeart Ltd, 95/G. and V. Chapman, 101/Steve Niedorf, 107/DC Productions

Impact Photos: 10 and 24 l/Jacqui Spector, 137/Mark Henley

Dr Lily Kyan: 93

Panos Pictures: 103/Sean Sprague

Christal Sheffield: 73

Frank Spooner Pictures: 49, 80, 108/Gamma-Liaison, G. Williams

Tony Stone Worldwide: 75

The publishers have made every effort to trace all copyright holders, but if they have inadvertently overlooked any, they will be pleased to make the necessary arrangements at the first opportunity.